CHRIST IS RISEN

33 Daily Meditations on the Miraculous

KEVIN COTTER
and ABBY FREDRICKSON

Hallow

Copyright © 2023 Hallow, Inc.

All rights reserved. No part of this book may be reproduced or transmitted in any form or by in any means, electronic or mechanical, including photocopying, recording, or by any information storage and retrieval system, without the written permission of the Publisher, except where permitted by law.

Scripture quotations taken from *New Revised Standard Version Bible: Catholic Edition*, copyright © 1989, 1993 the Division of Christian Education of the National Council of the Churches of Christ in the United States of America. Used by permission. All rights reserved.

Printed in the United States of America

CONTENTS

	INTRODUCTION	1
DAY 1	SIXTY-ONE MINUTES	3
DAY 2	WHY DO PEOPLE SUFFER?	7
DAY 3	THE DAY THE SUN DANCED	11
DAY 4	THE STIGMATA	15
DAY 5	WITHOUT PUPILS	19
DAY 6	PROOF OF THE RESURRECTION	23
DAY 7	SHE'S NOT GOING TO MAKE IT	27
DAY 8	WATER THAT HEALS	31
DAY 9	A STUBBORN AGNOSTIC	35
DAY 10	I WANT TO GET UP!	39
DAY 11	BREAKING FREE	43
DAY 12	AN INEXPLICABLE MYSTERY	47
DAY 13	JESUS FEEDS	51
DAY 14	WINTER ROSES	55
DAY 15	GOD IS IN THE DETAILS	59
DAY 16	THE MIRACLE OF A RABBI	63
DAY 17	CHARBEL	67
DAY 18	LIKE A WHISPERY BREEZE	71
DAY 19	PRAY FOR YOURSELF	75
DAY 20	GOD'S FOOL	79
DAY 21	A THOUSAND PENNIES	83
DAY 22	UNEXPECTED PROTECTOR	87
DAY 23	A MISTAKE REVERSED	91
DAY 24	DO NOT BE AFRAID	95
DAY 25	MIRACULOUS LIGHTS	99
DAY 26	THEY HAVE NO WINE	103
DAY 27	THE SWEETEST MOMENT	107
DAY 28	I SAW HER! I SAW HER!	111
DAY 29	WE KNOW HE'S A SAINT	115
DAY 30	SACRED HEART	119
DAY 31	INTERRUPTED	123
DAY 32	THE MOST EXTRAORDINARY PERSON	127
DAY 33	MIRACLE MAN OF MONTREAL	131

DAY 1 SIXTY-ONE MINUTES

INTRODUCTION

Welcome to *Christ Is Risen: 33 Daily Meditations on the Miraculous*! Each meditation is a daily reminder that God is alive and present in our lives.

At Easter, we celebrate the awe-inspiring miracle of Christ's resurrection. This mystery proclaims that God died for us and then rose from the dead. This isn't just His victory, it's our victory as well.

But it can be hard to experience that God is alive in our lives.

Sometimes we don't feel His presence.

Sometimes we don't see His impact.

Sometimes we wonder if our prayers even matter.

Our challenges, our sufferings, and our questions often distract us or make us doubt that God exists.

But what if we could experience that God is alive?

That God is moving.

That God is real.

That's what this book is all about.

Maybe you've believed in God your whole life.

Maybe you don't believe in God at all.

Maybe you're somewhere in between.

Wherever you find yourself, join us for this journey to explore how we can see God alive in the world and in our own lives today.

Because the reality is this: If God is alive, it changes everything.

DAY 1 SIXTY-ONE MINUTES

SIXTY-ONE MINUTES

Prayer is helplessness casting itself on Power, infirmity leaning on Strength, misery reaching to Mercy, and a prisoner clamoring for Relief.
• VENERABLE FULTON SHEEN •

In 2010, Bonnie Engstrom was expecting her third child. As her due date approached, everything was going smoothly. Like she had with her other children, Bonnie decided to give birth at home with a midwife. On June 16 she went into labor. Everything went smoothly for several hours, but as the baby began to pass through the birth canal, the midwife realized the umbilical cord had developed a knot. The child's oxygen supply had been cut off. Upon arrival, tragically, the baby didn't move and didn't cry. He had no pulse. He was stillborn.

Bonnie and her friend present at the birth immediately began to ask Fulton Sheen to pray for the baby. Archbishop Fulton Sheen lived from 1895 to 1979. He was ordained a priest in 1919, and was well known for his television show, Life Is Worth Living, for which he won an Emmy. Bonnie had long been a fan of Archbishop Sheen, who had grown up in the same area of Illinois as she had.

While Bonnie and her friend prayed, the midwife gave the baby CPR, and the family called 911.

When the paramedics came to the house, they confirmed that the baby had no sign of a heartbeat.

They rushed him to the hospital. Upon arrival, the child still had no pulse.

On a sonogram, the child's heart still showed no movement.

The doctors asked that the baby receive five more minutes of care before declaring him dead.

After this time, the team took their hands off the child.

And it was then... at this moment... after sixty-one minutes without oxygen... that his little heart started beating.

No one can live without oxygen for sixty-one minutes, especially a newborn baby. The doctors expected severe organ failure. They didn't know how long he would live, maybe a night or a weekend, but certainly not a week. And yet the child continued to progress. While this was promising, the Engstroms were told that the best-case scenario would be that their child would have an extreme form of cerebral palsy. He would be blind, and he would never be able to walk, talk, or feed himself.

The requests for Archbishop Sheen's intercession continued. Bonnie, who kept a blog, wrote on the day of his birth that if the child lived, it would be the sole result of the intercession of Archbishop Sheen. Soon hundreds of people from around the world began to pray for the child.

Defying all odds, the child continued to grow and improve. To this day, against all scientific explanation, the child has developed normally and shows no signs of his traumatic beginnings. He is James Fulton Engstrom, named after his intercessor. In 2019, Pope Francis approved this occurrence as a miracle with attribution to the intercession of Archbishop Fulton Sheen. Venerable Fulton Sheen is now on the path to sainthood.

DAY 1 REFLECTION & MEDITATION

Is there an area of your life in which you feel helpless? Sick? Miserable? Imprisoned? Take this time now to bring these areas to prayer. How can you lean on and reach out to God today?

DAY 2 WHY DO PEOPLE SUFFER?

WHY DO PEOPLE SUFFER?

*God cares for you; only fear and distrust
on your part can thwart his good designs.*
• BLESSED SOLANUS CASEY •

Miracles can be inspiring, but they can also raise hard questions: Why does God heal some and not others? Why does He allow suffering to occur in the first place? The mystery of suffering comes through in a powerful way today as we hear about a priest who was given the miraculous power to heal while he himself suffered deeply.

Born on November 25, 1870, in Prescott, Wisconsin, Bernard Casey was the sixth of sixteen children. His parents, Irish immigrants, were successful farmers. In his mid-twenties, Bernard joined the Capuchins in Detroit, Michigan, and took the religious name Solanus. Although bright, he struggled in seminary because the classes were in Latin and German. To his humiliation, he was made a "priest simplex"—a priest who could say Mass but wasn't considered intelligent enough to hear confessions or preach. His jobs were menial ones: training the altar boys and answering the door.

Solanus would endure much worse suffering. He developed chronic quinsy, which made him feverish much of the time and caused pain and swelling in his throat. He had trouble with his sight and hearing. He developed and survived gangrene. In his seventies, he had psoriasis on his legs, which caused open, oozing sores that developed into cancer.

Despite these sufferings, Solanus was believed by those who knew him to be a saint. Not only did he exude a natural joy, but he also possessed a supernatural ability to heal others.

Solanus was so renowned for his ability to heal that his superiors ordered him to keep a notebook of prayer requests. While it became impossible to keep up this task during his eighteen-hour workdays, he did make six thousand entries during a twenty-one-year period of those who asked for prayers. These were entered into the Seraphic Mass Association, his order's prayer network. About one in ten has a follow-up entry, such as:

Russell Jay, seventeen years old ... 49 inches tall ... hadn't grown since he was five years old. A second entry appears six months later: *Today Russell Jay reported he grew four-and-a-half inches, and is now developing normally.*

Mrs. Mary E. Reynolds, 59, of Clinton, Ontario. Seventeen years with epileptic seizures. Enrolled three months ago. Has not had a shadow of an attack since.

John Charles Kulbacki, six years old. Blind since three weeks old; was enrolled in Seraphic Mass Association six weeks ago. On Christmas Day, when here at church, was almost frightened as he pointed to a light and exclaimed, "Look, Mama."

Cases like these fill Solanus's notebook, and many more stories fill books and archives—accounts of tumors and cancer being healed, vision being restored, and the crippled being able to walk again.

Despite healing so many, Solanus humbly admitted to those who came to him that he didn't have all the answers to the mysteries of suffering and illness. He once said plainly, "I don't understand why children have to suffer."

As a priest, despite the thousands of requests he received each year, he never refused to see anyone, whether it was the middle of the night or the one hundredth person that day. This was true throughout his life, even at the end when he suffered the most. During this time, he confided to a friend, "I looked on my whole life as giving, and I want to give until there is nothing left of me to give." He died on July 31, 1957, and was beatified in 2017.

DAY 2 REFLECTION & MEDITATION

Despite healing so many, Bl. Solanus was still troubled by the mystery of suffering. What suffering troubles you in your life? What fears and distrust do you have right now as a result of your suffering? Talk with God about it. Solanus asked that those requesting a miracle place their faith in God and thank him no matter the outcome. What act of faith can you make in light of the suffering and fear you face right now?

DAY 3 THE DAY THE SUN DANCED

THE DAY THE SUN DANCED

O My Jesus, forgive us our sins, save us from the fires of hell.
Lead all souls to Heaven, especially those in most need of Thy mercy. Amen.

One of the most extraordinary miracles in the history of the Church is "the miracle of the dancing sun"—an amazing event witnessed by more than seventy thousand people.

Our story begins in 1917 with three young children in rural Portugal: Lucia dos Santos, age nine, and two of her cousins, eight-year-old Francisco Marto and his six-year-old sister, Jacinta Marto. They grew up in a devout Catholic household in a small village with many members of their extended family.

The years leading up to this event were years of terror for those in the Catholic Church in Portugal. Priests and bishops had been imprisoned or exiled, religious orders were suppressed, and almost all the seminaries were closed.

It was amid this backdrop that Mary appeared to these three children on their way home from tending their flock of sheep. Mary told the children that she would appear on the thirteenth day of the month for the next five months.

As the months passed, word of Mary's apparitions to these three children spread. Although the children were the only ones able to see Mary, more and more spectators joined them on the thirteenth of each month. However, many in prominent positions questioned the validity of these events. Anti-religious newspapers ran biased and negative reports. The Portuguese government applied pressure on the children and their families. At one point, the local mayor even kidnapped the children and tried to bribe them before threatening them with death unless they recanted their testimony.

All of this came to a head when Mary promised the children that she would perform a miracle so that all would believe. With that news, the anticipation and controversy surrounding these events reached a fever pitch.

On October 13, the children prepared to meet Our Lady once again. This time they were joined by over seventy thousand people who had traveled from all over Portugal to join them, despite the torrential rains they encountered as they gathered.

As the children met with Mary and the people looked on, the incredible miracle occurred. The sun danced, changed colors, swirled, and descended toward the earth. The crowd, who previously had been covered in rain and mud, were left completely clean and dry. Physical cures of the blind and lame were reported, and the miracle was seen as far away as twenty-five miles by people who had no previous knowledge of the events.

Believers were amazed and nonbelievers were converted. Even one of Portugal's anti-religious reporters published a story attesting to the truth of the event. In spite of public criticism, the headline ran, "The Day the Sun Danced at Noon in Fatima."

The story of Our Lady of Fatima is one of the most profound and grand miracles in the history of the Catholic Church. Just like those who witnessed the actual event, we can stop and marvel at what the Lord did to bring more people to faith in Him.

DAY 3 REFLECTION & MEDITATION

Spend some time now talking with God. What is on your mind after hearing this story? What do you want to ask God for today? Take some time to lift up any intentions or anyone you want to pray for.

DAY 4 THE STIGMATA

THE STIGMATA

Suffering, no matter how difficult it may be, when compared to the good that is accomplished, makes every pain a joy for the soul.

• ST. PADRE PIO •

Today's meditation centers on a saint whose entire life was marked by extraordinary and supernatural signs. Theexceptional nature of these miracles is matched only by the science that analyzed and verified these events during his lifetime.

St. Pio Forgione, better known as Padre Pio, lived from 1887 to 1968. From a young age he had devoted himself to Christ, and he became a Capuchin friar of the Franciscan Order in Italy.

On September 20, 1918, after celebrating Mass in his monastery, San Giovanni Rotondo, Padre Pio lay prostrate in prayer. He suddenly saw a person with the wounds of Christ:

The sight of Him frightened me: what I felt at that moment is indescribable. I thought I would die and would have died if the Lord hadn't intervened and strengthened my heart which was about to burst out of my chest. The Person disappeared and I became aware that my hands, feet and side were pierced and were dripping with blood.

During this experience, Padre Pio was given the stigmata—Jesus' wounds on his hands, feet, side, and shoulder. Padre Pio wasn't the only saint to experience the markings of Jesus' crucifixion; St. Francis of Assisi, St. Catherine of Siena, and St. Faustina Kowalska all experienced the pain of Christ in various ways.

Padre Pio's wounds remained with him every day of his life. Thousands of people witnessed them at the Masses he celebrated, and his fellow friars had an up-close look at them daily.

The wounds in his hands were about the size of a quarter. They were transparent, and numerous reports mention that they were often accompanied by a sweet fragrance.

Because Padre Pio's wounds were visible in the age of scientific and medical advancement, they were examined and studied numerous times. Doctors marveled at the existence of his open wounds. Wounds such as these either heal and show scars or, if they fail to heal, become infected. Padre Pio's wounds did neither. The doctors who examined him noted that his wounds had unusually smooth edges and showed no signs of swelling or inflammation.

Some skeptics accused Padre Pio of causing the wounds himself through some type of chemical; others wondered if the wounds were created because of a psychological condition. But at the end of his life, fifty years after he first received the stigmata, the wounds disappeared entirely, leaving no scar or mark on his skin. The wounds that defied science during his lifetime continued to defy all explanation after his death as well.

Beyond the stigmata, Padre Pio's life was marked by extraordinary signs. There are numerous claims that he could bilocate—having the ability to be physically in one place and spiritually present in another. When he heard confessions, he had the ability to read souls and would recall in detail a particular sin that the person confessing had not shared. There also are many healing accounts associated with the friar, including raising the dead back to life, giving sight to the blind, and healing the crippled.

DAY 4 REFLECTION & MEDITATION

Spend some quiet moments with God now, beginning with this prayer from St. Padre Pio:

O Lord, we ask for boundless confidence and trust in Your divine mercy, and the courage to accept the crosses and sufferings which bring immense goodness to our souls and that of Your Church. Help us to love You with a pure and contrite heart, and to humble ourselves beneath Your cross, as we climb the mountain of holiness, carrying our cross that leads to heavenly glory. May we receive You with great faith and love in Holy Communion, and allow You to act in us as You desire for your greater glory. O Jesus, most adorable Heart and eternal fountain of Divine Love, may our prayer find favor before the Divine Majesty of Your heavenly Father. Amen.

DAY 5 WITHOUT PUPILS

WITHOUT PUPILS

*You must have boundless faith in the divine goodness,
for the victory is absolutely certain.*

• ST. PADRE PIO •

Gemma de Giorgi was born on Christmas day in 1939 in the Sicilian town of Ribera, and almost immediately, her mother knew something was wrong with her eyesight. She took her daughter to several doctors who determined that she was born without pupils. She would be blind for life, and there was no medical solution. Her parents, people of deep faith, began to pray for her miraculous healing at Mary's altar at their local parish.

One of their relatives was a nun, and she advised them to seek out Padre Pio, a renowned miracle worker, so the family asked her to write a letter to him. Sometime later, the nun saw Padre Pio in a dream in which the friar asked her, "Where is this Gemma for whom so many prayers are being offered that they are almost deafening?" In the dream, the sister introduced Gemma to Padre Pio, and he made the Sign of the Cross over her eyes. The very next day the nun received a letter in reply from Padre Pio. He wrote, "Dear daughter, rest assured that I will pray for Gemma. I send you my best wishes."

Upon experiencing the convergence of these events, the nun recommended that the family travel to see Padre Pio at his monastery, San Giovanni Rotondo. When the family was about halfway along the very long and difficult journey, something extraordinary happened. Gemma began to see for the first time. She looked out of the window of her train car and saw the ocean and a steamship passing by. Her parents, in shock, continued their fervent prayers.

After their arrival at San Giovanni Rotondo, they joined a large crowd waiting to see Padre Pio. The friar, in the midst of the crowd, singled out Gemma and called her by name. He heard her confession and traced the Sign of the Cross over her eyes with part of his hand affected by the stigmata. Later that day Padre Pio gave Gemma her first Holy Communion and again made the Sign of the Cross over her eyes.

When she returned to Sicily, a specialist examined her eyes. She still did not have any pupils. Physically, medically, scientifically... she was still blind. But, miraculously, she was able to see. The specialist held up various objects in front of her, and she could see each of them. She could count how many fingers he was holding up from a distance of sixteen feet. She went on to live a normal life, and her eyesight continued to improve.

Throughout her life, various doctors have examined Gemma's eyes and time after time have confirmed that, despite all scientific explanation, she is able to see without pupils. At the time of this writing, Gemma de Giorgi is still alive. You can see videos of this remarkable woman online.

DAY 5 REFLECTION & MEDITATION

What stood out to you from Gemma's miraculous story? Use this to start a conversation with God. In what ways do you need God's help to see more clearly?

DAY 6 PROOF OF THE RESURRECTION

PROOF OF THE RESURRECTION

"If Christ has not been raised, your faith is futile and you are still in your sins. Then those also who have fallen asleep in Christ have perished. If for this life only we have hoped in Christ, we are of all people most to be pitied."

• 1 CORINTHIANS 15:17–19 •

If Jesus truly rose from the dead, then eternal life is possible. If not, then, as St. Paul notes, we should be pitied because of the time and energy we've wasted in living our lives for Jesus. The Resurrection is the hinge on which Christianity either stands or falls. That's why our miracle today—The Shroud of Turin—is so important.

The Shroud of Turin, kept in Turin, Italy, since the sixteenth century, is believed by many to be one of the two burial cloths of Jesus. The cloth contains full-body images of a man—one of his entire front side and the other of his back from head to toe. The image was somehow burned onto the cloth, showing a man's body with the markings of one who has been crucified.

This image has been revered by the Church for centuries but came to attention in a new way with the use of modern-day photography in the late nineteenth century. When pictures were taken, the photographic negatives revealed a lifelike, more detailed image.

At this time, the Shroud gained worldwide attention. People wanted to know if it was the real burial cloth of Jesus or just a medieval hoax.

Here are some of the findings that scientists discovered in the last few decades:

The image reveals a man who was crucified in a unique way that matches Jesus' crucifixion. The image contains marks on his hands and feet, as well as wounds on the man's side, several wounds on the head that match the crowning of thorns, and numerous wounds on the back that match the scourging at the pillar.

The image contains 120 unique bloodstains. This pattern perfectly matches those found on what is believed to be the second burial cloth of Jesus, held today in Oviedo, Italy. Bloodstains on the cloth have tested positive for human blood components, and the blood is type AB—the rarest blood type. This is also the blood type found on the second burial cloth in Oviedo and in the Eucharistic miracles of Lanciano and Buenos Aires.

Much of the controversy around the cloth centers around whether it is truly from the time of Jesus or if it was made in medieval times. Scientists found that the image contains pollen species that date back to the first century from plants common only in Israel. The most recent carbon dating of the cloth in 2013 dates it between 300 BC and AD 400.

Scientists have found that the shroud is definitively not the product of an artist. It contains no paint, ink, dye, pigment, or stain. It seems to have been created by an intense burst of ultraviolet radiation. Not only did the ancient world not have access to this kind of technology, but we also don't have this kind of technology today. Scientists have shown that in order for the Shroud not to have been destroyed by fire through the heat generated, the image would have to have been made instantaneously. Believers often point to the cause of such an occurrence as the moment of Jesus' Resurrection.

All this evidence has made the Shroud one of the most compelling miracle stories in the history of the world. While the Catholic Church has not made an official declaration on the authenticity of the Shroud, the evidence for the Shroud continues to astound believers and nonbelievers alike.

If these miracle stories are true—if Jesus really did rise from the dead—are you willing for this to change the way you live? The way you think? Take a few moments to consider two or three ways you want to live differently.

DAY 6 REFLECTION & MEDITATION

Read St. Paul's image of the final resurrection in 1 Corinthians 15:51–58. Let it fill you with hope, knowing that whether you witness a great miracle or a thousand small ones in your lifetime, Jesus' Resurrection has thrown open the doors of heaven for each of us, and that will always be the greatest and most awe-inspiring miracle of all.

DAY 7 SHE'S NOT GOING TO MAKE IT

SHE'S NOT GOING TO MAKE IT

Do not look forward to what may happen tomorrow; the same everlasting Father who cares for you today will take care of you tomorrow and every day. Either He will shield you from suffering, or He will give you unfailing strength to bear it. Be at peace, then, put aside all anxious thoughts and imaginations, and say continually: "The Lord is my strength and my shield; my heart has trusted in Him and I am helped. He is not only with me but in me and I in Him."

• ST. FRANCIS DE SALES •

In October 2006, twelve-year-old Avery Gerleman scored a goal in a soccer game. Instead of celebrating, though, she headed for the sideline and threw up blood. She was rushed to the hospital in Wichita, Kansas.

At the hospital, the news was not good. All of Avery's organs were failing, most notably her kidneys and lungs. Her blood vessels were disintegrating. For days, doctors had no idea what was killing Avery. One doctor remarked, "She's not going to make it, no matter what we do." The doctors informed Avery's parents, Shawn and Melissa, that Avery was going to die.

During these chaotic days, Shawn and Melissa turned to their Catholic faith. Shawn begged for the intercession of Fr. Emil Kapaun, a Kansas farm kid turned US Army chaplain and Korean War hero. Shawn wrote in his journal, "Father Kapaun, take all the prayers said for Avery this week and lay them at the feet of the Lord. Intercede and obtain a miracle for Avery, her full and immediate recovery for the Greater Glory of God."

Shawn had a good reason to turn to Kapaun. Born in rural Kansas in 1916, Kapaun became a priest before joining the military as a chaplain. During the Korean War, Kapaun's battalion of a few thousand US troops was bombarded by twenty thousand Chinese soldiers. Kapaun raced between foxholes and past the front lines into no-man's-land. He dragged the wounded to safety, heroically risking his life despite commands for evacuation. The US battalion was defeated, and the soldiers were led on a death march to their POW camp in North Korea.

While in captivity, Kapaun saved hundreds of men. He foraged for food, made pots to boil water, washed and cleaned wounds, and gave his own clothes to soldiers. He led the soldiers in prayer and said Mass in secret. One soldier remarked, "That faith is what kept us alive."

Kapaun suffered various tortures from his captors. When his health finally deteriorated, he was taken to the "death house." He was last seen blessing and forgiving his captors. In 2013, President Barack Obama awarded him the Medal of Honor, making him the most decorated chaplain in the history of the United States.

Thousands across Kansas, the United States, and the world prayed for Avery and asked for Fr. Kapaun's intercession. Doctors finally identified the root of Avery's deteriorating health: pulmonary-renal syndrome, an autoimmune disorder that causes the body to attack itself. A radical treatment plan was put into place. Doctors still believed she would die, and if she somehow survived, they thought she would live in a vegetative state for the rest of her life. But against all odds, Avery began improving. She regained consciousness, dispelling the fear of a vegetative state. Her kidneys showed no scarring and very little tissue damage. Six months later, Avery was playing competitive soccer again. All of this completely baffled her doctors.

In 1993, thirteen years before Avery's traumatic experience, Emil Kapaun was named Servant of God after he was found to have lived a virtuous and heroic life. Next, a miracle was needed to move him along the path to canonization and name him a saint. Vatican officials came to Kansas to interview Avery and her family. The two doctors who oversaw Avery's case, both non-Catholics, passionately told a Vatican official—with tears in their eyes—that there was no scientific explanation for what happened. Later the official would tell Avery's parents that in all his years of poking holes in miracle stories, he had never heard a story as persuasive as the one told by Avery's doctors.

Today, Fr. Emil Kapaun remains a Servant of God, and the Vatican continues to examine his case for sainthood.

DAY 7 REFLECTION & MEDITATION

Reflecting on what had happened to her after being healed, Avery wondered, "Why did God choose me?"

Have you ever felt this way after experiencing God's blessings? Have you ever wondered the opposite when it seems that God is ignoring your suffering and not answering your prayers? Jesus' life, death, andRresurrection give meaning to our struggles. How might God use your suffering to bring you closer to him?

DAY 8 WATER THAT HEALS

WATER THAT HEALS

I shall spend every moment loving. One who loves does not notice her trials; or perhaps more accurately, she is able to love them. I shall do everything for Heaven, my true home. There I shall find my Mother in all the splendor of her glory. I shall delight with her in the joy of Jesus Himself in perfect safety.

• ST. BERNADETTE •

In a small French village, a fourteen-year-old girl named Bernadette was collecting firewood by a stream on a cold February day in 1858. Suddenly there was a rush of wind. As Bernadette looked up, she saw standing above her in the grotto a young woman wearing a white dress with a blue sash and white veil. Yellow roses were at her feet, and in her hands she held a rosary.

Bernadette felt an inexplicable sense of happiness and peace. She knelt down, reached into her pocket for her own rosary, and started to pray with the woman. When she finished, the young woman disappeared.

Up until that moment, Bernadette had lived a life of obscurity and poverty. Frequently sick, she often couldn't attend school. She couldn't read, and she had never learned enough to be able to receive her first Holy Communion.

Over the next few months, Bernadette would see the woman eighteen times. Word spread, and many thought she was vying for attention. Bernadette and her family suffered ridicule, but she continued to return to the grotto. Each time more people joined her, first out of fascination and then out of devotion. Although only Bernadette could see the woman, those with her could not deny the peace they felt in the grotto.

On February 25, the woman told Bernadette to drink water from a spring that flowed under her. Bernadette was confused; there was no spring in sight.

She started to dig with her hands, and the crowd that had followed her there watched with interest. She dug and dug, but nothing happened. The crowd started to laugh at this young girl covered in dirt—who did she think she was? She was clearly out of her mind.

But the next day, Bernadette returned to the grotto to find water flowing. Joyfully Bernadette drank and washed in it, inviting the crowd that had laughed at her to join her. Shocked, they did, and many were miraculously healed in this spring that continues to flow to this day.

On March 25, the woman finally told Bernadette her identity: "I am the Immaculate Conception."

Bernadette had no idea what this meant, and when she shared it with her parish priest, he was shocked. How could an illiterate, uneducated girl know about the Immaculate Conception, Mary's title that asserts she was born without original sin—a teaching that had only recently been defined and accepted by the Church? This convinced many that what Bernadette had seen really had come from God, and in 1862, the Church acknowledged the authenticity of the apparitions.

Bernadette joined the Sisters of Charity and returned to a life of obscurity and illness, never being healed of her physical ailments herself and dying in her thirties. When her body was exhumed in 1909, it was found to be incorrupt, miraculously defying the normal process of decay after death.

Today, millions of people go to the grotto at Lourdes every year. They go to pray, wash their bodies in the spring, and open their hearts to God. Over the next few days, we'll pray with a few of the many miracles that have taken place at Lourdes.

DAY 8 REFLECTION & MEDITATION

Today, how can you "spend every moment loving," as Bernadette aspired to? Take a few moments to imagine yourself in Heaven, beside your Mother. Like Bernadette, let your heart delight "in the joy of Jesus Himself" and dwell "in perfect safety."

A STUBBORN AGNOSTIC

Prayer is the most powerful form of energy one can generate.... It supplies us with a flow of sustaining power in our daily lives.
• ALEXIS CARREL •

What happens when a hardened agnostic, Nobel Prize–winning doctor witnesses two incredible miracles before his own eyes? This is the story of Alexis Carrel.

In 1894, an assassin stabbed Sadi Carnot, the president of France. The knife severed one of his major arteries, and doctors were unable to save him. That same year, Alexis Carrel was in his third year of medical school. He became determined to figure out a way to suture ruptured blood vessels, a discovery that would save countless lives. Over the next eight years, he worked on this problem until his revolutionary paper in 1902 presented a solution. He received international fame and later won a Nobel Prize for his work.

In 1902, a colleague asked Alexis to go to Lourdes on a white train—a special train designed to take the sick to the shrine. Alexis had grown up in a devout Catholic home but had fallen away from his faith. He decided to go to Lourdes because he wanted to study and question the authenticity of the miracles reported there.

On the same train was a woman named Marie Bailly, who was dying from acute tuberculosis; her stomach was distended with large, hard masses. White trains to Lourdes did not permit those near death to make the trip, but a sympathetic nurse managed to get her on board moments before the train departed from Lyon.

Alexis encountered Marie on the train. She was half-conscious, and he believed she would pass away soon after arriving at Lourdes, if not before.

By the time they arrived at Lourdes, Marie was in a coma. With Alexis accompanying her, a pitcher full of Lourdes water was poured three times on Marie's abdomen.

Alexis wrote in his notes, "The enormously distended and very hard abdomen began to flatten and within thirty minutes, it had completely disappeared. No discharge whatsoever was observed from the body."

Marie Bailly made full recovery.

Because her cure was so rapid, complete, and inexplicable, it became public news in France and throughout the world. Secular reporters drummed up controversy, claiming that Alexis witnessed the events but did not believe it was a miracle. Alexis replied that some believers were too quick to make miraculous claims, while others in the medical community refused to look at the possibility of a miracle. Alexis's openness to the very idea that a miracle was possible was very controversial in the French scientific community—so much so that Alexis lost his job.

Although still agnostic, he continued to make trips to Lourdes. On another occasion, he witnessed and attested to the healing of an eighteen-month-old blind child. And yet, Dr. Alexis Carrel still did not convert.

It would take thirty-six years from the time he witnessed Marie's miracle until Alexis found faith. Several years before his conversion, he became friends with a Trappist monk, Fr. Alexis Presse. The two began a dialogue, and after four years, Alexis shared that he believed in God, the immortality of the soul, and the teachings of the Catholic Church.

Just two years later, Alexis lay dying in bed and sent for Fr. Presse to administer the final sacraments— Penance, the viaticum, and Anointing of the Sick. He died a faithful Catholic.

DAY 9 REFLECTION & MEDITATION

When we hear the story of Dr. Alexis Carrel, it can be easy to scoff at his lack of faith despite witnessing two miracles. Yet have there been times in your life when God has clearly shown you His love—and you failed to let it change your life? Is there anything you struggle to believe in? Never be afraid to bring your struggles and doubts to God, and never stop praying.

DAY 10 I WANT TO GET UP!

I WANT TO GET UP!

Holy Mary, Mother of believers,
Our Lady of Lourdes, pray for us. Amen.
• FROM A PRAYER OF POPE ST. JOHN PAUL II •

In December of 1899, Gabriel Gargam was a thirty-year-old office clerk for the French postal service. As he traveled on the express train from Bordeaux to Paris, Gabriel's train collided with another train at the speed of fifty miles per hour. Gabriel was launched from the train and landed fifty-two feet away from the wreckage. He lay unconscious in the snow, bruised and broken, for seven hours before he was taken away on a stretcher, barely alive.

Over time, the formerly large man wasted away to a skeleton, weighing only seventy-eight pounds.

His feet became gangrenous.

He was unable to eat solid food.

He was unable to help himself, even in the smallest of ways.

Two trained nurses assisted him day and night. His family filed a lawsuit against the railroad, and doctors testified that he would be crippled for life. Some described his condition as a living death.

Gabriel had grown up in a faithful Catholic home, but by the time he reached the age of fifteen, he had lost his faith. Prior to the accident, he hadn't been to church for fifteen years. After his accident, his aunt, a religious sister of the Order of the Sacred Heart, begged him to go to Lourdes, but he refused. His mother continued her appeals for months, but he turned down each request. Finally, after two years of pleading, Gabriel agreed to go.

At this point, Gabriel hadn't left his bed since the accident. When they left for the trip, they carried him on a stretcher to the train. The exertion caused him to faint, and he was unconscious for an entire hour afterward. On the way to Lourdes, it looked as if Gabriel would die along the way. The family considered abandoning their plan, but Gabriel's mother insisted that they go on.

When they arrived at Lourdes, Gabriel went to confession and received Holy Communion, but his condition remained the same. He was taken to the baths at Lourdes, but to no effect. In fact, when he went to the baths, the exertion again caused him to faint. When he didn't revive, his family feared that he had died. Sorrowfully, Gabriel's family placed a cloth over his face and began to travel back to the hotel with whom they believed to be their dead son.

On their way back, they saw a Eucharistic procession. As the priest passed by carrying the Sacred Host, he gave them a blessing. Suddenly, the cloth covering Gabriel's face began to move. Then the body once thought to have passed away rose up to a sitting position. As the family looked at Gabriel in amazement, he spoke in a full and strong voice: "I want to get up!"

His family believed Gabriel was in some sort of delirious state caused by his impending death. They tried to soothe him, and eventually they tried to hold him down, but he broke free. Gabriel got up and walked away. After walking a few paces, he turned back to his family, proclaiming, "I'm cured!"

By this time a crowd had surrounded them, watching in awe. Gabriel's family and those who gathered fell to their knees and thanked God for his miracle.

The man who could not get out of bed could now walk.

The man who had needed two nurses to do everything for him day and night could now do everything on his own.

The man who had to be fed from a tube now sat down at a table and ate a hearty meal.

Gabriel's case was so famous that in August of that year, sixty doctors came to examine him in one day. They all pronounced him entirely cured.

While Gabriel's physical cure was miraculous, he was spiritually healed as well. He and his wife dedicated themselves to Mary Immaculate. He consecrated himself to the service of the sick, returning each year to Lourdes. In 1951, on the fiftieth anniversary of his miraculous cure, Gabriel Gargam sat in a chair at Lourdes surrounded by fifty thousand pilgrims while his story was proclaimed to the crowd. He died a couple of years later at the age of eighty-three.

DAY 10 REFLECTION & MEDITATION

Gabriel's family didn't give up on him; they continued to seek his healing and draw him back to the faith. Who are the people who have helped you in your faith journey? As you name them, give thanks to God for the ways they have shared His love with you.

Are there any people close to you who do not believe or no longer believe in God? Take some time now to pray for the people who come to mind. Lifting all these people to God's merciful love, close by asking Mary for her intercession as you pray a Hail Mary.

DAY 11 BREAKING FREE

BREAKING FREE

Ever-Immaculate Virgin, Mother of Mercy, health of the sick, refuge of sinners, comforter of the afflicted, you know my wants, my troubles, my sufferings; look with mercy on me. Our Lady of Lourdes, pray for me!

• PRAYER TO OUR LADY OF LOURDES •

John Traynor, a native of Liverpool, England, had been an active combatant in numerous World War I battles and, as a result, had a number of debilitating injuries. His right arm was paralyzed, and the muscles had atrophied. His legs were partially paralyzed, and he suffered from epilepsy. He had undergone a host of operations on his arm and brain, all leaving him worse than before. He now had a one-inch hole in his head with a silver plate shielding his brain.

In 1923, John heard that the Liverpool diocese was organizing a pilgrimage to Lourdes. His Irish mother had raised him Catholic, and he had always had a great devotion to the Blessed Virgin Mary. John's wife and friends tried to talk him out of going. His doctor said it could kill him to go. Even the priest leading the pilgrimage begged him not to come. But John was determined to go to Lourdes.

During the trip, John became very sick. Several times the directors of the pilgrimage tried to take him off the train, but there was no hospital nearby. John's condition was so bad upon arrival in Lourdes that a woman on the trip wrote to his wife, saying there was no hope for him and that he'd be buried in Lourdes.

The nurses and caregivers in Lourdes didn't want to take him to the baths for fear he would die along the way. As they started to head toward the baths, John suffered a seizure, so his nurses turned back. John used his good hand to stop his wheelchair and wouldn't let go until they took him. He continued to go back to the healing baths of Lourdes again and again during his first three days there.

After his ninth time in the baths, he started to feel what he described as agitation in his legs. He tried to get to his feet, but his nurses wouldn't let him. Then, during the Eucharistic procession, he was touched by the monstrance and experienced an agitation in his withered arm. Although he had lost the use of his arm eight years earlier, he now burst all of his bandages and was able to make the Sign of the Cross.

Early the next morning, John heard the bells of the basilica ringing. He jumped out of bed and knelt on the floor to finish his Rosary. Then he ran out of his room. Despite being only 112 pounds, he pushed two of the caregivers aside, slid past a doctor, and ran barefoot on a gravel path to the Grotto. The caregivers ran after him but couldn't catch up. They found John on his knees thanking Our Lady in gratitude.

An interesting element of this story is that John didn't really realize what had happened to him. It wasn't until a conversation with the Archbishop of Liverpool on the way home that everything sunk in.

The Archbishop asked, "John, do you realize how ill you have been and that you have been miraculously cured by the Blessed Virgin?" In his own words, John Traynor said:

> *Suddenly, everything came back to me, the memory of my years of illness and the sufferings of the journey to Lourdes and how ill I had been in Lourdes itself. I began to cry, and the Archbishop began to cry, and we both sat there, crying like two children.*

News of Traynor's miracle spread quickly and articles were published in the Liverpool papers. A great number of conversions in Liverpool resulted from the miracle, including John's two caregivers and their families, who were Protestant at the time.

Three years later, John was examined, and it was found that his cure was permanent. His arm, the muscles of which had all withered away, had recovered completely. The gaping one-inch hole in his head from the surgery had completely disappeared. And his epilepsy completely ceased. None of John's issues ever returned.

DAY 11 REFLECTION & MEDITATION

Have you ever asked Our Lady of Lourdes to pray for you? Take a moment now to share the intentions that are on your heart.

AN INEXPLICABLE MYSTERY

God dwells in our midst, in the Blessed Sacrament of the altar.
• ST. MAXIMILIAN KOLBE •

August 18, 1996, began as a normal Sunday. Fr. Alejandro Pezet celebrated Mass at St. Mary's Church in Buenos Aires, Argentina. As he finished distributing Holy Communion, a woman approached him and told him that she had found a discarded host on the ground. Fr. Pezet followed the normal protocol in this situation—he placed the host in distilled water so it could dissolve.

Eight days later, on Monday, August 26, when the tabernacle was opened, to everyone's amazement, the host had turned into a bloody substance. The priest notified his auxiliary bishop, Bishop Jorge Bergoglio (the man who would become Pope Francis). Bishop Bergoglio gave the instructions for the host to be professionally photographed. The photographs clearly showed that the host had become a fragment of bloodied flesh and had grown significantly in size. The host then remained in the tabernacle.

After several years, the host was sent off for analysis. During a five-year period, the host received a number of tests from several experts. In order to not prejudice the study in any way, the scientists were not told where the sample came from or why it needed to be examined.

Dr. Frederick Zugibe, a cardiologist and forensic pathologist, summed up the findings:

The substance is real flesh and blood containing human DNA.

Specifically, the material is a fragment of the heart muscle found in the wall of the left ventricle close to the valves.

This piece of heart muscle is in an inflammatory state and contains a large number of white blood cells. Since white blood cells cannot live outside of a living organism, this finding indicates that the heart was alive at the time the sample was taken.

Furthermore, Dr. Zugibe found that the white blood cells had penetrated the tissue. This indicated that the heart had been under great duress and that the owner had been beaten severely in the chest. Dr. Zugibe told the research team to notify the police because a violent crime had most likely occurred.

When informed that the substance came from a consecrated host that was kept in distilled water for three years, Dr. Zugibe was dumbfounded. He stated: "How and why a consecrated host would change its character and become living human flesh and blood will remain an inexplicable mystery to science—a mystery totally beyond her competence."

In addition to these findings, the sample came back with blood type AB positive—one of the rarest blood types. AB positive is both a universal recipient (meaning it can receive blood from any blood type) and a universal plasma donor (meaning its plasma can be given to anyone). This same blood type has been identified in various Eucharistic miracles, including the blood type found on the Shroud of Turin.

This Eucharistic miracle completely confounds all scientific and medical explanation. A piece of bread turned into a living piece of heart tissue despite being contained in distilled water for several years, coupled with the particularities of the tissue, point directly to the only person who could be responsible for its occurrence: the crucified Christ.

DAY 12 REFLECTION & MEDITATION

How does this miraculous story strengthen your faith? How might it change the way you receive Communion the next time you go to Mass? Spend a few quiet moments now thanking God for the gift of Jesus in the Eucharist.

DAY 13 JESUS FEEDS

JESUS FEEDS

I want to be the boy who offered everything he had. It was nothing, five loaves and two fish, but it was "everything" he had, which he gave up to be an instrument of the love of Jesus.
• VENERABLE FRANCIS XAVIER NGUYEN VAN THUAN •

Imagine you've been following Jesus for a while now. His words and miracles have begun to stir both excitement and controversy, and you've witnessed things you never imagined possible. As you continue on your journey, you find yourself on a boat with Jesus, crossing to the other side of the Sea of Galilee.

As the boat nears the shore, you see thousands of people waiting for a chance to meet this Jesus, hoping for a chance to experience the healing power they've heard of.

Can you picture it? It's a huge crowd, larger than any you've ever seen. You come ashore, climb up a mountainside, and find a place for Jesus to sit. You're on crowd control, encouraging the people to come one by one to Jesus. The air buzzes with anticipation and joy as people are healed and comforted.

Jesus calls you and the other disciples over and asks how you plan to feed everyone. Philip quickly responds: "Six months' wages would not buy enough bread for each of them to get a little!" But out of obedience you go in search of food, and Andrew finds a boy with five loaves of bread and two fish. It's all you can offer to Jesus.

Jesus nods at what you have to offer and tells you to order the crowd to find a place to sit.

You've followed him long enough to know not to argue. You tell everyone to sit down. Maybe you feel a little ridiculous and worry about what people will think of you. People ask you what is happening, but you don't have an answer. You just tell them that Jesus wants to feed them.

Once everyone is seated, you walk back to Jesus. He takes the five loaves and the two fish, and looking up to heaven, he says the blessing, breaks the loaves, and gives each of you pieces to go out and share with the people.

Now you really feel on the spot. As you give bread to the first row of people, you are peppered with questions from others in the rows behind: "What about us? Will there be enough? What's going on?"

All too soon, you are out of bread and fish and only a few people have been fed. Avoiding the eyes of the crowd, you hurry back to Jesus. When you get there, he hands you more bread and more fish. He smiles at your amazement.

You go back to the people, pass out the food, and return. Once again, Jesus hands you more bread and more fish. Your hesitating walk turns into a joyful run; you're grinning, racing to bring more food to the people. And each time you come back to Jesus, there is more bread and more fish.

When everyone has eaten, Jesus instructs you: "Gather up the fragments left over, so that nothing may be lost." Together with the other disciples, you gather twelve baskets full.

DAY 13 REFLECTION & MEDITATION

Today, Jesus asks us to feed those around us, to be his hands and feet in the world. This call can feel hard to live up to. Maybe we are worried about what people will say. Maybe we are afraid of being humiliated. Maybe we don't feel like we have that much to offer. But Jesus looks at our hesitations and worries and meager offerings and says, "I can work with that." He takes what we have and multiplies it to the point of overflowing.

Who in your life is Jesus asking you to feed, either physically or spiritually? Are you willing to be put on the spot—or even humiliated for Jesus? Share with God what feelings this brings up for you.

DAY 14 WINTER ROSES

WINTER ROSES

"Am I not here, I, who am your Mother? Are you not under my shadow and protection? Am I not the source of your joy? Are you not in the hollow of my mantle, in the crossing of my arms? Do you need anything more? Let nothing else worry you or disturb you."

• OUR LADY OF GUADALUPE •

Today's story begins in 1531, in a small village near what is now Mexico City. It had been a little more than ten years since Spain had conquered Mexico, bringing Christianity to the region. Juan Diego, an indigenous Mexican, was in his fifties. He and his wife had recently converted to Catholicism, and on one ordinary December day, he was walking to his catechism class.

As Juan passed over a hill, he heard strange music. Turning, he saw a woman. She addressed him in his own language, Nahuatl, and revealed to him that she was the "true mother of the true God." She gave Juan a challenge: Go to the bishop and request that a chapel be built in her honor.

Stunned, Juan went to Bishop Juan de Zumarraga and shared his experience. The bishop listened attentively and then asked for proof.

Juan returned to the hill and again saw the woman. This time, he begged her to send someone else—perhaps someone of higher standing who could be more persuasive. But she replied that she had chosen him to be her messenger, and again she entrusted him with the same message. Juan obediently went to the bishop again, but the bishop insisted on concrete proof.

When Juan relayed this message to Our Lady, she told Juan that the next time they met—December 12—she would give him a sign that would convince the bishop.

But on that day, Juan's uncle became gravely ill. Rather than return to meet Our Lady, Juan went to find a priest to give his uncle last rites. He took a route that avoided the hill, not wanting to be delayed from reaching the priest. But Our Lady appeared to him on his journey and gently chastised him for not trusting her. She said:

Am I not here, I, who am your Mother? Are you not under my shadow and protection? Am I not the source of your joy? Are you not in the hollow of my mantle, in the crossing of my arms? Do you need anything more? Let nothing else worry you or disturb you.

She instructed Juan to change direction, climb the hill, and pick the roses he would find in bloom. Humbled, Juan did so, and Our Lady placed these roses in Juan's tilma, or cloak, and told him to take them to the bishop.

Standing before the bishop, Juan opened his tilma and the flowers fell on the ground. The bishop and those who were present with him were amazed to see flowers in the middle of winter, but the true shock was Juan's tilma—impressed upon it was an intricate image of Our Lady, with stars above her head and the moon beneath her feet.

Those in the room were in awe. Convinced that Juan Diego had indeed seen the Blessed Virgin, the bishop immediately began plans to build a chapel in her honor.

Juan Diego then returned home to find his uncle cured.

Over the next ten years, nine million people converted to Catholicism because of Our Lady's incredible miracle. Juan spent the rest of his life living next to the chapel built for Our Lady of Guadalupe, which is now the most visited shrine in the world.

DAY 14 REFLECTION & MEDITATION

Our Lady of Guadalupe is a reminder of God's love for us; He knows we need a mother to lean on and lead us to Him. Hear Mary speaking to you the same words she spoke to Juan Diego. Is there anything you wish to share with her? What worries can you place in her hands?

DAY 15 GOD IS IN THE DETAILS

GOD IS IN THE DETAILS

O Virgin of Guadalupe, you want to remain with us through your admirable Image, you who are our Mother, our health, and our life. Placing ourselves beneath your maternal gaze, and having recourse to you in all our necessities, we need do nothing more. O Holy Mother of God, despise not our petitions, but in your mercy hear and answer us.

• FROM THE MEMORARE TO OUR LADY OF GUADALUPE •

In our story yesterday, we learned about Our Lady of Guadalupe and Juan Diego. Modern science has discovered some amazing details about Juan Diego's tilma, and these details attest to the truth behind this miracle.

After Our Lady's image appeared on the tilma, Juan Diego carried it from town to town, sharing his story and bringing people to faith in God. Then, it was permanently displayed at the newly built shrine. For 115 years it had no protection—many hands touched it, and it was exposed to soot, candle wax, and incense.

The image on the tilma should have faded away, and the tilma itself should have rotted and disintegrated. Replicas of tilmas with the same chemical and structural composition last only fifteen years before decomposition. But now the tilma is almost five hundred years old and shows very little sign of wear. Its very existence is a miracle.

Some of the details on the tilma were added later, including the angels, moon, and rays of light. These were hand-painted on the cloth, and they are degrading. In contrast, there is no degradation at all of the original image.

Dr. Philip Callahan of NASA has stated, after extensive testing of the cloth, that the original image reveals no brush strokes or signs of human design (such as under-sketches). The image is smooth and feels like a modern-day photograph, though it was produced three hundred years before the invention of photography. This evidence points to the original image being created in a single moment.

Nobel Prize–winning biochemist Richard Kuhn stated that the pigments from the original image are not from any known natural source on earth, whether animal, mineral, or vegetable. Yet there were no synthetic pigments in use anywhere in the world in 1531.

The eyes of Our Lady have been studied by multiple eye doctors, and they all agree that under a microscope, the eyes appear to be human rather than a created artistic image.

Dr. José Aste Tonsmann, an engineer, magnified the pupil's image 2,500 times and discovered an image of thirteen people, believed to be Bishop Zumarraga and the others in the room when Juan Diego opened his tilma. The distortion of the image is perfectly accurate to the natural curvature of the eyeball; it's exactly how a human eye would reflect an image. No one could have painted this in 1531—there wasn't even the technology to observe this minuscule image at that time.

There are other incredible details of the tilma as well:

The stars on Our Lady's mantle accurately reflect what the sky would have looked like on December 12, 1531, in that part of the world.

A Mexican accountant, Fernando Ojeda, viewed the flowers and stars in the image as if they were musical notes and discovered a beautiful melody. Analysts repeated the experiment with copies of paintings from the sixteenth and seventeenth centuries, where stars and flowers had been placed at the painter's discretion, but the only thing they produced was "noise, not harmony."

The rich symbolism within the image itself shared the Gospel story with the people who looked on it. Our Lady appears to be mestizo, a blend of Spanish and indigenous heritage, symbolizing she is for all peoples.

The tilma reminds us that God cares about the details. He loves to delight and surprise us. And He wants all people to know Him.

DAY 15 REFLECTION & MEDITATION

What are some ways God has surprised and delighted you lately? How does Juan Diego's tilma deepen your faith and encourage your heart?

DAY 16 THE MIRACLE OF A RABBI

THE MIRACLE OF A RABBI

Today the Lord repeats to me, to you: Follow me! Waste no time in questioning or in useless chattering; do not dwell on secondary things, but look to what is essential and follow me. Follow me without regard for the difficulties. . . . Follow me by speaking of me to those with whom you live, day after day, in your work, your conversations and among your friends. Follow me by proclaiming the Gospel to all, especially to the least among us, so that no one will fail to hear the word of life which sets us free from every fear and enables us to trust in the faithfulness of God. Follow me!

• POPE FRANCIS •

One of the great mysteries isn't that God works miracles, but that He chooses to work miracles through human beings. God wants to show us that He's alive, and He's willing to work through us along the way. In today's story, we hear of one of Jesus' most famous miracles. The startling part is not what it says about Jesus, but what it says about us.

In the Gospel of Matthew, Jesus instructs his disciples to go to the other side of the lake while He goes off to pray. While they are crossing the sea of Galilee during the middle of the night, the disciples see a man who appears to be walking on the water. What would you think if you were in a boat in the middle of the night and saw someone walking on water?

Fortunately, Matthew captures their reaction in all of its glorious detail: "But when the disciples saw him walking on the sea they were terrified. 'It is a ghost,' they said, and they cried out for fear." You can almost see how much Matthew enjoys telling people about the time he and his friends freaked out that night. Eventually, the disciples recognize the man as Jesus. Peter, in his usual bold way, steps up and says, "If it is you, Lord, tell me to come out on the water."

Put yourself in Peter's shoes. It's the middle of the night. A man is walking on water. And your first reaction is: *Maybe I should do it too!* Peter is a special kind of person, but he's also doing what he was trained to do. You see, the whole goal of a disciple was to follow their rabbi and to learn to be like them. Jesus is the rabbi, and Peter is his disciple. Peter puts his training into practice, despite the absurdity of this situation. You can see the wheels turning in Peter's head: *If my rabbi can walk on water . . . that means . . . THAT I CAN WALK ON WATER!*

And sure enough, Jesus says, "Come."

Matthew tells us what happens next: "So Peter got out of the boat and walked on the water and came to Jesus; but when he saw the wind, he was afraid, and beginning to sink he cried out, 'Lord, save me.' Jesus immediately reached out his hand and caught him, saying to him, 'O man of little faith, why did you doubt?'"

Everyone remembers Jesus' part of the miracle. And we often focus on the fact that Peter sinks. But the true miracle is that Peter also walks on water. Even though he's human, he not only tries to walk on water, but he actually does it . . . until he is too afraid.

This is the ultimate lesson Jesus has for us today.

If you follow Jesus, you, too, are his disciple. You, too, are called to walk in his footsteps. Even when you fail, even when you are weak, even when you think you can't do it, Jesus will be there to help you. Jesus believed in His first disciples and chose them to carry out His mission despite their sins and weaknesses. He'll do the same with you as his disciple today.

DAY 16 REFLECTION & MEDITATION

Reread the quote from Pope Francis. How do his words challenge and encourage you? What can you do today to leave your doubts behind and step out boldly in Jesus' footsteps? As you sit quietly with Him, hear Him say, "Take courage, it is I; do not be afraid."

DAY 17 CHARBEL

CHARBEL

God knows our whole being. Those who ask for His grace with confidence will not be disappointed. Ask Him to give you all you need.
• ST. CHARBEL MAKHLOUF •

In 1993, Nohad El Shami suddenly suffered severe weakness, stiffness, and lack of control in her left leg, arm, and mouth. A mother of twelve, she was fifty-five years old at the time and living in Lebanon just north of the Holy Land. She was immediately taken to the hospital for tests. Nohad was diagnosed with hemiplegia, a condition caused by an obstruction of arteries in her brain. The doctors concluded that recovery was unlikely because no treatment for her condition existed.

Upon hearing this news, her son rushed to Saints Peter and Paul Hermitage, the former home of St. Charbel Makhlouf, a monk and hermit born in 1828 in Lebanon. St. Charbel became a monk at twenty-three, a priest at thirty-one, and a hermit at forty-six. As a hermit, he lived a life of intense prayer and fasting. During his lifetime, he was known for several miracles and healings. Upon his death, there were many miraculous signs and wonders associated with him, including the fact that his body remained incorrupt after death. Pilgrims flocked to his tomb and prayed for his intercession. There were many reports of healings and answered prayers.

Following this tradition, Nohad's son, Saad, brought back consecrated oil and soil from the hermitage to give to his mother.

Shortly after, Nohad was released from the hospital, but her health did not improve. She spent several days in constant, agonizing pain. But then, one night she had a dream that she attended Mass at St. Charbel's hermitage and St. Charbel himself gave her Communion. Next, she had a second dream. In it, two monks were standing by her bed. One monk operated on her neck while the other monk held a pillow behind her back to support her.

When Nohad awoke, she could move her arms and legs and walk normally. Her hemiplegia was completely healed. It was a miracle! Nohad also discovered something that was out of the ordinary, even for stories about miracles. She had two thin, surgical incisions on her neck. These incisions were several inches in length.

The following night, Nohad had one more dream involving St. Charbel. The saint told her, "I did the surgery to let people see and return to their faith. I ask you to visit my hermitage on the 22nd of every month and attend Mass regularly."

Since this miracle, a movement of prayer has developed around the world on the 22nd of each month. The monks at Saints Peter and Paul Hermitage have welcomed thousands of pilgrims and have received up to two hundred thousand people on St. Charbel's feast day. They've documented hundreds of thousands of accounts about St. Charbel's effective intercession, and devotion to St. Charbel continues to grow.

DAY 17 REFLECTION & MEDITATION

What stood out to you from this miracle story?

As a saint in heaven, St. Charbel is a powerful intercessor. He can bring our prayers to God and pray for us—just as we would ask a friend to pray for us. As you think of your own needs and the needs of those around you, what might you consider asking St. Charbel to intercede for on your behalf?

DAY 18 LIKE A WHISPERY BREEZE

LIKE A WHISPERY BREEZE

Dear Jesus, help me to spread Your fragrance everywhere I go.
Flood my soul with Your spirit and life.
Penetrate and possess my whole being so utterly,
That my life may only be a radiance of Yours.

• ST. JOHN HENRY NEWMAN •

In 1989, Marion Carroll was asked a question that completely changed her life. Jerry, her ambulance driver, asked her: "Would you like to go to Our Lady of Knock?"

During the previous fifteen years, Marion's health had greatly deteriorated. The mother of two was in her late thirties and suffered from multiple sclerosis. For the last few years, she was completely bedridden or confined to a wheelchair. She had lost all power in her legs and her right arm. She was almost blind and her speech was slurred. She had no control over her bowel and bladder, and she wore a neck brace because she could no longer support her head. She also suffered from epilepsy, thyroid problems, and a kidney infection. Marion was slowly dying, and there was no cure. She was completely dependent on her husband, Jimmy, for even the most basic needs.

Knock was the location of a Marian apparition, and it was located fifty miles north of Marion's home. Though she was a devout Catholic, Marion had no desire to go there. She had been to Knock once years before and thought it was a miserable place. But eventually she was persuaded to go with a group of friends while her husband stayed at home with their children.

In Knock, Marion was strapped on a stretcher and taken to Mass at the basilica on-site. While she was there, she didn't pray for herself, but for her husband, knowing that her death would be difficult and painful for him. During Communion, Marion felt a sharp pain in her heels, unlike anything she had felt before. As the pain in her heels went away, so did the pain in the rest of her body. At the end of Mass, the bishop brought the Eucharist within a monstrance right in front of her stretcher. When he held the monstrance up and blessed her, Marion described feeling "a beautiful feeling, a magnificent feeling, like a whispery breeze telling me ... that I could get up and walk."

After the Mass, Marion was nervous to share her experience, but she finally mentioned it to a friend. Her friend undid the straps on her stretcher, and her legs swung out. Marion stood up and began to walk. She was able to support her own head and could use her hands and legs. Even after three years of being in a wheelchair, she wasn't stiff, and her muscles worked fine. Her slurred speech was now coherent. However, what Marion remembers most is the joy and peace she felt at that moment.

Jimmy was waiting for her at home. When the ambulance arrived, she let him push her wheelchair inside. Then she stood up and said, "Jimmy, I can walk."

Jimmy fell to his knees and wept. He had believed she was going to die soon and often prayed that the Lord would cure her and take him instead.

In September 2019, thirty years after her cure, the Catholic Church officially recognized Marion's experience as a miracle. Marion remains in good health today. She leads a ministry of healing and travels throughout the world, giving testimony to God's love. She says, "My healing in Knock does not belong to me. This is a special gift to let people know that Jesus and Mary are there."

DAY 18 REFLECTION & MEDITATION

Marion could not keep her experience of God's grace to herself. She recognized it as a gift to help others believe that God is real. We, too, are called to share our own experiences of God's love and mercy with others.

How might God be calling you to give witness to His love? As you go through your day, look for opportunities to spread His love to every soul you come in contact with.

DAY 19 PRAY FOR YOURSELF

PRAY FOR YOURSELF

God has created me to do Him some definite service; He has committed some work to me which He has not committed to another. I have my mission.

• ST. JOHN NEUMANN •

In 1891, Mary Catherine Monroe was a widow who lived in Philadelphia, Pennsylvania. The fifty-year-old former schoolteacher was stricken with uterine tumors and could barely walk across her boardinghouse room. The doctors told her that she would die, and the Catholic convert occupied her time preparing for a happy death.

One day, Mary Catherine was visited by Mrs. Clayton, one of her Protestant friends, with an urgent request. She explained: "My sister is dying. I've heard miracles can be obtained by praying at your Bishop Neumann's tomb. I want to go there and pray, but I don't know how one acts in a Catholic place. Won't you please come with me?"

Mary Catherine let her friend know that she would normally be happy to accompany her, but there was no way she could go in her feeble state. Mrs. Clayton was prepared for an answer like this and had arranged for three friends to help carry Mary Catherine.

The friends set off for the tomb of the former Bishop of Philadelphia. His story sheds light on why these women were so determined to visit his grave.

During the nineteenth century, thousands of religious men and women from Europe left their homes to serve immigrants in the Americas. One of these was John Neumann.

St. John Neumann was born in 1811 in Bohemia, in the present-day Czech Republic. While he was in seminary, he felt called to be a missionary and made his way to the United States. He was ordained a priest and joined the Redemptorists. After serving as a parish priest, he was appointed the Bishop of Philadelphia.

During his time as bishop, he faced anti-Catholic riots and arson of religious buildings, but he dedicated his life to building churches and schools (nearly one a month!), making Catholic education available throughout the diocese. He intervened to save the Oblate Sisters of Providence—a congregation of African American women—from dissolution, and he actively supported religious orders to come and teach in diocesan schools.

In 1860, at the age of forty-eight, he collapsed in the street and died. While no miracles were known during his lifetime, many were attributed to his intercession soon after his death. Word spread, and many Catholics visited Neumann's tomb asking for prayers.

His renowned intercession led Mrs. Clayton to ask her dying Catholic friend to help her pray for her sister. As they interceded for Mrs. Clayton's sister, Mary Catherine suddenly heard a gentle voice instruct her, "Now pray for yourself."

Immediately a strange thrill passed through her body, so strange that Mary Catherine believed she was dying. In fact, the opposite had happened. She was healed.

The same woman who had been carried by her friends down to the tomb now leaped up the steps and walked back to her boardinghouse. She remained vibrantly healthy from that day until she died, a decade later, still cancer-free. But that wasn't the only miracle that had taken place. Mrs. Clayton's dying sister was also healed. She went on to live an additional five years.

In 1977, almost eighty years later, Bishop John Neumann was canonized a saint. This story and numerous other miracles were submitted for Neumann's cause for canonization.

DAY 19 REFLECTION & MEDITATION

St. John Neumann lived selflessly and with great zeal. Like him, we each have a mission given to us by God. Ask the Risen Christ to show you how to live—and pray often for others as well as yourself.

DAY 20 GOD'S FOOL

GOD'S FOOL

A cheerful and glad spirit attains to perfection much more readily than a melancholy spirit.

• ST. PHILIP NERI •

Philip Neri was born in Florence, Italy, in the sixteenth century. From a young age, he was known for being cheerful and gentle, earning him the nickname "Good Little Phil." At eighteen years old, Philip went to live with a wealthy family member in the hopes of eventually taking over the business. But while there, he had a profound spiritual experience that changed his life.

Philip lost interest in owning property and instead felt a call to radically serve Jesus Christ and His Church. He left everything and went to Rome with nothing but the clothes on his back.

When Phillip arrived in Rome, he found a city full of corruption. Clergy and laity alike had stopped living like Christians. For the next sixteen years, Philip dedicated himself to prayer, serving the poor, and numerous friendships around the city, including with St. Ignatius of Loyola and St. Francis Xavier. During his life, Philip was an advisor to bishops, cardinals, and kings. He also lovingly ministered to prostitutes and those in hospitals.

People loved Philip for his wisdom and humor. Despite having access to so many prominent people, Philip didn't take himself too seriously. In fact, he often went to incredible lengths to prevent others from having good opinions of him. He would walk around in large white shoes or dress in bizarre outfits whenever he thought he'd meet cardinals. He would wear his clothes inside out or shave half of his beard. He truly wanted to be God's fool. His good humor and friendly manner won people over.

When he was twenty-nine, Philip was praying for the gifts of the Holy Spirit in the catacombs in Rome on the eve of Pentecost. During his prayer, he saw a globe of fire enter his mouth and fall into his heart. He immediately felt a sense of physical heat. He exclaimed, "Enough, enough, Lord, I can bear no more." He took off his shirt and threw himself on the ground to cool himself. He placed his hand over his heart and discovered a swelling as large as his fist. He could hear loud heart palpitations, but they caused him no pain. Philip went to the doctor, and he found that two of Philip's ribs were broken and arched outward. His heart had become unusually large, but there was no sign of disease. The doctors believed that the cause of the phenomenon was a miracle.

A few years after this mystical experience, Philip was ordained to the priesthood. Several times, he could have become a cardinal, but instead, he formed an oratory where priests lived a common life dedicated to serving God and His people.

Philip Neri lived an additional fifty years, and he continued to hear palpitations from his enlarged heart for the rest of his life, particularly when he was praying, hearing confessions, offering Holy Mass, and distributing Holy Communion. Those who heard the palpitations said they sounded like blows of a hammer.

He died at the age of eighty, and just twenty-seven years after his death, he was canonized a saint.

DAY 20 REFLECTION & MEDITATION

What (or who) brings you joy? How does your joy—or the lack of joy—affect others? How does it affect your relationship with God? Today, ask God to help you see Him as the source of all joy.

A THOUSAND PENNIES

I will willingly abandon this miserable body to hunger and suffering,
provided that my soul may have its ordinary nourishment.
• ST. KATERI TEKAKWITHA •

In 2006, Jake Finkbonner was playing the final game of his kindergarten basketball season. When the five-year-old went for a layup in the last minute of the game, he was pushed from behind and hit his lip on the base of the basketball hoop. At first his parents thought it was nothing, but overnight, his face swelled profusely, and he developed an intense fever. A day later, he was hospitalized.

The doctors diagnosed him with Strep A, a flesh-eating bacteria that was spreading across Jake's face. One of Jake's doctors described it as "lighting one end of a parchment paper, and you just watch it spread from that corner very fast, and you're stamping it on one side, and it's flaming up on another." The chief of plastic surgery at Seattle's Children's Hospital said he had never seen a case so dire. Each day the surgeons removed more and more of his skin in order to stay ahead of the infection, but it was still moving too fast.

The doctors told Jake's parents, Donny and Elsa, several times that their son would probably die. Recalling these moments, Elsa said, "Donny and I went off to the chapel and just surrendered Jake back to God. We just said, 'God, he is yours. Thy will be done, and if it is your will to take him home, then so be it.'" His parents called their priest, Fr. Tim Sauer, to come pray with them. They desperately prayed for a miracle and asked others to do the same. Fr. Sauer recommended that the family pray through the intercession of Blessed Kateri Tekakwitha.

Kateri Tekakwitha was a Native American who lived in North America from 1656–1680. From a very young age, Kateri developed smallpox that severely scarred her face and weakened her eyesight. At the age of nineteen, she converted to Catholicism and eventually moved from upstate New York to Canada, where she devoutly practiced the faith and pursued a life of holiness. During her lifetime, many considered her to be a saint. In her early twenties, Kateri passed away. Just fifteen minutes after her death, the scars on her face disappeared. Additional miraculous occurrences happened shortly after her passing, and many people began asking for her intercession. In 1980, she was beatified by the Catholic Church.

Jake and Bl. Kateri shared multiple similarities. Both Jake and Kateri are of Native American descent. Both suffered from a disease that disfigured their faces, and both were very young when their diseases started.

People from around the world began to pray for Jake's healing. Sr. Kateri Mitchell, the executive director of the Tekakwitha Conference, heard about Jake's case and flew to Seattle to be with the family. She brought a relic of Bl. Kateri, placed it on Jake's leg, and prayed with his family, asking for Kateri's intercession.

At this point, Jake's doctors hadn't expected him to make it through the night. The following morning, Jake was taken into surgery in a last-ditch effort to save his life. After only forty-five minutes, the doctors asked to meet with Jake's parents. Donny and Elsa believed they would be told that their son had died.

The doctor began, "I don't know how to tell you this, but it stopped. There's nothing there. It's like this volcano has been erupting for weeks and all of a sudden it has stopped."

Everyone was stunned—everyone, that is, except maybe Jake. Because soon after his recovery he recounted having an out-of-body experience the night before his miraculous recovery. He remembered hearing the voices of his family and doctors and his body starting to feel lighter; when he opened his eyes, he found himself in what he thought was heaven. He met his grandmother who died before he was born and his uncle who had died just two weeks before. Eventually, he encountered Jesus, who gave him a hug and whose heart entered Jake's body. When it was time to return, he said it sounded like a thousand pennies falling from the sky, and he found himself back in his hospital bed.

DAY 21 REFLECTION & MEDITATION

Jake spent an additional two months recovering in the hospital and received countless surgeries to repair the scarring on his face little by little. The Vatican approved his miraculous recovery as a sign of Bl. Kateri's intercession, and Jake's miracle helped prompt her canonization.

On October 21, 2012, Kateri Tekakwitha was declared a saint, with twelve-year-old Jake, his parents, and his sisters in Rome for the celebration. Jake is a constant reminder to his community of God's healing power.

Take your intentions to St. Kateri and ask that she take them to the foot of the Cross. Implore her to ask Jesus to bring healing to those who are heavily burdened. Pray with confidence that God's healing power is still at work today.

UNEXPECTED PROTECTOR

Do not put off till tomorrow the good you can do today. You may not have a tomorrow.
• ST. JOHN BOSCO •

The year was 1852; the place, Turin, Italy.

St. John Bosco, affectionately called Don Bosco, was at the time still a young priest. In Turin, he witnessed many young boys fall into the juvenile detention system, and he dedicated himself to teaching and serving children who were homeless or disadvantaged. He developed teaching methods based on love rather than punishment, and while he was beloved among the poor, he faced persecution and threats from those who hated Catholics. His work often involved walking the streets at night, placing him in dangerous situations.

One night as he was walking, a large gray dog appeared. At first, Don Bosco thought it was a wolf, and he was afraid. But the animal wagged its tail and joined him as he walked back to his mother's house, where they sheltered boys who did not have a home. When he reached the house, the dog trotted off in the direction from which it had come.

Every night from then on, when Don Bosco was out late, he found the dog waiting for him whenever he had to walk through a dangerous part of the town. Don Bosco named the dog Grigio, meaning "gray one."

One night, two men were following Don Bosco, matching their pace to his. When he tried to avoid them by crossing the road, they crossed too. He started to run, but they threw a cloak over his head. He struggled to free himself and call for help, but it was useless. Suddenly, with a howl, Grigio appeared out of nowhere. Leaping on the man who held the cloak, Grigio forced him to let go, then he bit the second man and flung him to the ground. Grigio stood over them both, growling.

"Call off your dog!" they cried to Don Bosco.

"I will call him off if you will let me go in peace," he replied.

"Yes, anything! Just call him off!"

"Come, Grigio," said Don Bosco, and the dog immediately obeyed. The two men ran off, terrified.

Another night, instead of accompanying Don Bosco, Grigio went to his house and refused to let him go out, lying down across the door of his room.

Don Bosco gave in at last, and fifteen minutes later, a neighbor came to warn him that he had overheard two men planning to attack him.

Stories spread of these incidents, and Don Bosco and his faithful friend became famous in the city. The boys whom Don Bosco cared for loved Grigio and wanted him to live with them, but Grigio never stayed for long. And then one day, he disappeared. Ten years passed. It seemed Grigio was gone forever.

Then one night, Don Bosco was out walking late and was filled with fear. "I wish I had Grigio here," he said to himself. And suddenly, Grigio appeared, wagging his tail. He walked the whole way with him and protected Don Bosco when two dogs tried to attack him. When they arrived safely at their destination, Don Bosco's friend went to bring Grigio some food. But the dog was gone, this time never to be seen again.

DAY 22 REFLECTION & MEDITATION

If you are reading this in the morning, think about the day ahead. If it is evening, think about your day tomorrow. What do you have planned? Is there anything you are excited or nervous about? Walk through your day with God and ask Him to cover you with His protection.

What are one or two ways you can follow in St. John Bosco's footsteps and purposely do good in thought or action? What intentions can you offer to God throughout the day today or tomorrow?

DAY 23 A MISTAKE REVERSED

A MISTAKE REVERSED

I will go anywhere and do anything in order to communicate the love of Jesus to those who do not know Him or have forgotten Him.

• ST. FRANCES XAVIER CABRINI •

In 1921, at New York City's Columbus Hospital, a nurse named Mae Redmond made her last round amidst the newborn babies she was caring for. As she picked up a whimpering child, she gasped. Peter Smith, born just two hours earlier, was burnt and disfigured. His eyes had a deep and grotesque swelling.

Panicked, she recalled her care since the child's birth. She had weighed and measured him and put drops in his eyes as prescribed by law. She went back to the bottle she used, only to realize that the formula was a 50 percent silver nitrate solution. Typically only 1 percent silver nitrate solution is used for a baby's eyes.

To put this in context, a 5 to 25 percent solution is used to eliminate something like a tumor. A 50 percent solution is strong enough to put a hole in a piece of wood. Mae cried out in terror, and soon four different doctors, including Dr. Horan, an eye specialist, checked on the child. The last doctor exclaimed, "Anything stronger than 1 percent solution and that's a blind baby."

Mother Teresa Bacigalupo, superior of the sisters who ran the hospital, pleaded with the doctors to do something to save Peter's sight, but one doctor responded, "Nothing short of a miracle can help this kid." So Mother Bacigalupo declared, "Then we will pray."

The Missionary Sisters of the Sacred Heart that Mother Bacigalupo was a part of had been founded by Mother Frances Cabrini. In the late nineteenth century, Cabrini dreamed of being a missionary to China. But when she met with Pope Leo XIII, he asked her to care for the immigrant populations that had moved to America. During her missionary work, Mother Cabrini established schools, hospitals, and orphanages throughout North America—sixty-seven institutions in all. She had died just three years earlier.

Mother Bacigalupo, her sisters, and Mae Redmond spent all night in prayer in the chapel, asking Mother Cabrini to intercede for Peter. At 9:00 a.m. the next morning, Dr. Horan returned to check on Peter. Surprisingly, the baby's eyelids were much less swollen. He pulled back Peter's eyelids to see how the acid had ravaged his eyes. But to his amazement, he found two perfectly healthy eyes staring back at him. The horribly charred skin from the day before was already healing and once again becoming the smooth skin of an infant.

Just seventeen years later, Mother Cabrini was beautified by the Catholic Church. As a seventeen-year-old, Peter attended the ceremony at St. Peter's, and onlookers could see his clear eyes and his smooth skin. Only those who knew his story well could notice the two small scars on his cheeks as tiny signs of the accident.

Years later, Peter Smith became a priest, and until his death in 2002, he loved to talk about Mother Cabrini and how her intercession changed his life.

DAY 23 REFLECTION & MEDITATION

When all hope felt lost, Mother Bacigalupo, the sisters, and Mae Redmond all spent the night in prayer. It was, in a sense, their own Garden of Gethsemane. Like Jesus, they looked to the Father when the suffering felt too great to bear.

Are there any hardships in your life that you wish God would relieve you from? Perhaps a difficult relationship, a tough scenario at work, a health issue, or loneliness? Use this opportunity to bring your suffering to God and keep your eyes on Him.

DAY 24 DO NOT BE AFRAID

DO NOT BE AFRAID

Why should we have no fear? Because man has been redeemed by God. When pronouncing these words in St. Peter's Square, I already knew that my first encyclical and my entire papacy would be tied to the truth of the Redemption. In the Redemption we find the most profound basis for the words "Be not afraid!":
"For God so loved the world that he gave his only Son."

• POPE ST. JOHN PAUL II •

In April 2011, Floribeth Mora, a forty-seven-year-old business owner from Costa Rica, awoke with an excruciating headache. Her pain was so bad she had to go to the hospital. The doctors told her it was just a severe migraine, but after three more days of immense pain, she returned to the hospital. Additional tests revealed an alarming discovery: Floribeth had an aneurysm on the right side of her brain, and it was hemorrhaging.

Aneurysms, if not discovered in time, can be deadly. The problem with Floribeth's aneurysm was that the doctor didn't believe he would be able to operate. After consulting with experts across Latin America and Spain, it was determined too tricky and too perilous to attempt an operation. Having no other choice, the doctor sent her home. While aneurysms can occasionally exist without causing harm for several years, the bleeding indicated that her death was imminent.

In the aftermath of her diagnosis, Floribeth clung to her Catholic faith. She insisted on participating in a religious procession and believed she received a sign during this time that she would be healed. Her family also built an altar outside of her house. There she displayed a picture of Mary and a photo of Pope John Paul II, surrounded by colorful candles, Christmas lights, and flowers.

Pope John Paul II had died six years earlier in 2005, and his beatification was fast approaching.

On May 1, 2011, just twenty-three days after her first headache, Floribeth gathered her family around her bedside to watch Pope John Paul II's beatification on TV. On her bedside table was a magazine with John Paul on the cover. Floribeth recalls:

> *I contemplated the photo of the Holy Father with his arms extended and I fixed my eyes on him. In this moment, I heard a voice tell me, "Get up, don't be afraid," and I could only say, "Yes, I'm going to get up."*

Despite being afraid that her family would think she was out of her mind, Floribeth did get out of bed. And she immediately felt better.

Doctors confirmed what Floribeth already believed—medical exams showed that the aneurysm was gone. Over time, both Church and medical officials thoroughly researched Floribeth's case. In June 2013, Floribeth was told that her miracle had been chosen for the canonization of Pope John Paul II as a saint.

DAY 24 REFLECTION & MEDITATION

What fears do you have in your life right now? What anxieties do you face? Take a few moments to imagine yourself at the foot of the Cross and speak to Jesus about these fears and anxieties. Give them to the Lord and place all your trust in His love. Then simply meditate on these words: "Do not be afraid."

DAY 25 MIRACULOUS LIGHTS

MIRACULOUS LIGHTS

Our Lady of Knock, Queen of Ireland, you gave hope to your people in a time of distress and comforted them in sorrow. You have inspired countless pilgrims to pray with confidence to your divine Son, remembering His promise, "Ask and you shall receive, seek and you shall find."

• PRAYER TO OUR LADY OF KNOCK •

On August 21, 1879, eleven-year-old Patrick Hill was working at his aunt's house in a very small village in rural Ireland. At eight o'clock in the evening, a man named Dominick Byrne came into the house and cried out: "Come up to the chapel and see the miraculous lights, and the beautiful visions that are to be seen there." Patrick quickly joined Dominick and several others, and they began running to the nearby chapel.

As the group turned a corner, they saw the lights on the gable wall of the church. The lights spread from the ground up to the window of the building and higher. The lights were always consistently bright, but they changed in height as the group that had gathered looked on in awe. Later everyone in the group reported that they witnessed the same sight: an apparition of the Blessed Virgin Mary, St. Joseph, St. John, and an altar with a lamb on it and a cross behind the lamb.

Here is Patrick's vivid account after they arrived at the chapel:

It was raining.... After we prayed a while, I thought it right to go across the wall and into the chapel yard. I brought little Curry [a five-year-old] with me; I went then up closer; I saw everything distinctly. The figures were full and round as if they had a body and life.

Patrick went on to describe what Mary looked like:

> *I distinctly beheld the Blessed Virgin Mary, life-size, standing about two feet or so above the ground clothed in white robes which were fastened at the neck.... She appeared to be praying.... She wore a brilliant crown on her head, and over the forehead where the crown filled the brow, a beautiful rose; I saw her eyes, the balls, the pupils, and the iris of each. I went up very near; one old woman went up and embraced the Virgin's feet, and she found nothing in her arms and hands; they receded, she said, from her.*

Then Patrick went on to describe St. Joseph:

> *I saw St. Joseph to the Blessed Virgin's right hand; his head was bent, from the shoulders, forward; he appeared to be paying his respects; I noticed his whiskers; they appeared slightly grey ... I saw the feet of St. Joseph, too. His hands were joined like a person at prayer.*

Patrick also described St. John:

> *[He] was dressed like a bishop preaching; he wore a small mitre on his head; he held a Mass Book, or a Book of Gospels, in his left hand; the right hand was raised to the elevation of the head ... he appeared as if he were preaching, but I heard no voice; I came so near that I looked into the book. I saw the lines and the letters. St. John did not wear any sandals.*

Finally, Patrick described the altar, the lamb, and the angels:

> *The altar was a plain one, like any ordinary altar, without any ornaments. On the altar stood a lamb, the size of a lamb eight weeks old—the face of the lamb was fronting the west, and looking in the direction of the Blessed Virgin and St. Joseph. Behind the lamb a large cross was placed erect or perpendicular on the altar. Around the lamb I saw angels hovering during the whole time, for the space of one hour and a half or longer; I saw their wings fluttering, but I did not perceive their heads or faces, which were not turned to me. For the space of an hour and a half we were under the pouring rain; at this time I was very wet; I noticed that the rain did not wet the figures which appeared before me, although I was wet myself. I went away then.*

DAY 25 REFLECTION & MEDITATION

While this is Patrick's official testimony, various witnesses confirmed what he saw. Patrick was one of the fifteen people, ranging in age from five years to seventy-four, who witnessed the apparitions. Most of them gave an official testimony to the validity of these apparitions soon after the events just like Patrick. Throughout the course of their lifetimes, none of them changed their testimonies. Eventually, the Catholic hierarchy in Ireland formally approved the apparitions as worthy of devotion. Because these events happened in Knock, Ireland, in County Mayo, Mary was given the name "Our Lady of Knock," and the place of her apparition remains a pilgrimage site to this day.

Remember that we are all pilgrims on the road to Heaven. Ask Our Lady of Knock to fill you with love and concern for your brothers and sisters in Christ, especially those who live with you. Ask her to comfort you when you are sick, lonely, or depressed and give you a greater love for Jesus in the Blessed Sacrament.

DAY 26 THEY HAVE NO WINE

THEY HAVE NO WINE

Remember, O most gracious Virgin Mary, that never was it known that anyone who fled to thy protection, implored thy help, or sought thine intercession was left unaided. Inspired by this confidence, I fly unto thee, O Virgin of virgins, my mother; to thee do I come, before thee I stand, sinful and sorrowful. O Mother of the Word Incarnate, despise not my petitions, but in thy mercy hear and answer me. Amen

• THE MEMORARE •

John's Gospel takes us to a familiar setting: a wedding. Jesus has just begun to invite disciples to follow him when they are all invited to a wedding along with Mary, Jesus' mother. The wedding was in Cana, in Galilee, just over four miles from Nazareth.

The story begins with a problem—they run out of wine. Running out of wine would have been mortifying for the families hosting the wedding. This provokes a short but very interesting conversation between Jesus and Mary:

When the wine gave out, the mother of Jesus said to him, "They have no wine." And Jesus said to her, "Woman, what concern is that to you and to me? My hour has not yet come." His mother said to the servants, "Do whatever he tells you." (John 2:3–5)

Mary appears to make a request out of concern for the families involved. Jesus seems to rebuff her. And Mary responds by moving forward anyway. What's happening?

While Mary makes a simple observation, Jesus knows what she's asking—we need a miracle to help these people! Jesus turns her down, saying his hour has not yet come. Jesus' "hour" refers to His passion and death. Jesus knows that if He performs a public miracle, His ministry will begin and eventually lead to his death.

But Mary proceeds anyway. And Jesus obeys her.

Jesus directs the servants to fill six stone jars that hold twenty to thirty gallons of water. Jesus then turns the water into wine. Usually, the good wine is served first and then lesser quality wine is served as the night progresses, but to the surprise of the headwaiter, this is the best wine anyone has drunk all night.

In Jewish culture, wine was a symbol of life and God's blessing. By changing water into wine, Jesus hinted at what was to come—that His presence would turn suffering into joy, death into new life. And, like the new wine tasting richer than the old, Jesus follows a long line of God's servants in the Old Testament, but they all point to Him, the beloved Son of God.

Because of His mother's urging, Jesus performs this miracle. He creates overabundance out of scarcity. His public ministry has begun.

DAY 26 REFLECTION & MEDITATION

As the Queen Mother, Mary has a powerful role in interceding for us. Where in your life do you see areas of scarcity? Ask Mary to change that scarcity to abundance!

DAY 27 THE SWEETEST MOMENT

THE SWEETEST MOMENT

O Mary, conceived without sin, pray for us who have recourse to thee.
• INSCRIPTION ON THE MIRACULOUS MEDAL •

Zoe Labouré was born on May 2, 1806, in a quaint village in Burgundy, France. She was the ninth of eleven children in a farming family. At the age of nine, Zoe's mother passed away. When she returned from the funeral service, Zoe went to her room. She stood on a chair, took a statue of Our Lady from the wall, kissed it, and said, "No,w dear Lady, you are my mother."

At the age of twenty-three, Zoe joined the Daughters of Charity, a religious order of sisters founded by St. Vincent de Paul, and she received the name Sr. Catherine. A year later, she woke up in the middle of the night and heard her name being called three times. When she opened the curtains of her room, she saw her guardian angel in the form of a five-year-old child. He asked her to follow him to the chapel where the Virgin Mary would meet her.

Sr. Catherine dressed quickly and followed him. In the chapel, she didn't see the Virgin Mary, so she knelt and prayed for thirty minutes. Then her guardian angel said, "There is the Blessed Virgin Mary." Sr. Catherine knelt in front of the Mother of God, with her hands resting on Mary's knees. This began a two-hour conversation that Sr. Catherine would later call "the sweetest moment of my life." The Virgin Mary told Sr. Catherine that God had chosen her for a mission, but she would have to experience many difficulties along the way. She encouraged Sr. Catherine by telling her, "To those who will pray to Mother Mary, she will bestow her graces to all, rich and poor, to everyone who asks with confidence and fervor."

Four months later, in November 1830, Mary appeared to Sr. Catherine again in the same chapel. Sr. Catherine saw the Virgin Mary standing on a globe. She had light streaming from her outstretched hands, and framing the apparition was an inscription: "O Mary, conceived without sin, pray for us who have recourse to thee." Mary asked Sr. Catherine to create a medal with her image on it and to give it to every person she met. She promised that those who wore it would receive great graces, especially if it was worn around the neck. Those who repeat the inscription as a prayer would be under the protection of Mary in a special way.

With the approval of her spiritual director and archbishop, the first medals were made in 1832. These medals, originally called Mary's Immaculate Conception, were distributed during a deadly cholera epidemic in Paris that claimed over twenty thousand lives. Many cures and conversions were reported during this period and shortly thereafter. Over time the medal was commonly called the Miraculous Medal and over ten million medals were given or sold during the first five years. During the next forty-six years, Sr. Catherine knew about countless miracles, but she chose to remain anonymous until just before her death. At the time of her death, more than a billion medals had been made and were being distributed all over the world.

When Sr. Catherine's body was exhumed fifty-seven years later, it was completely incorrupt and lifelike. On May 28, 1933, she was beatified by Pope Pius IX, and on July 27, 1947, she was canonized St. Catherine Labouré by Pope Pius XII. Countless miracle stories have come through the Miraculous Medal and the power of Mary's intercession. We'll encounter one of these stories tomorrow.

DAY 27 REFLECTION & MEDITATION

The Miraculous Medal is not a superstition or a good-luck charm but a tangible reminder of Mary's promises and an opportunity to entrust ourselves to the power of Mary's intercession. Do you have a Miraculous Medal? If not, why not get one and begin wearing it? Who else in your life might benefit from this powerful reminder?

DAY 28 I SAW HER! I SAW HER!

I SAW HER! I SAW HER!

Our Lady of the Miraculous Medal, pray for us.

Marie-Alphonse Ratisbonne was born the eleventh of thirteen children on May 1, 1814, into a French family of wealthy Jewish bankers. When Alphonse was young, his older brother Théodore converted to Catholicism and became a priest. As a result, his family refused to speak with him ever again, and Alphonse developed a very negative attitude toward Catholics.

In his late twenties, everything in Alphonse's life seemed to be going in the right direction. He was engaged to be married and would become a partner at his uncle's bank. But before his wedding, he decided to travel around Europe.

During his time in Rome, he ran into one of his old Protestant classmates, Gustavo de Bussières. As they rekindled their friendship, Alphonse also met Gustavo's older brother, the Baron Théodore de Bussières. The baron was a convert to Catholicism and a close friend of Alphonse's estranged brother.

The baron made it his mission to convert Alphonse. He gave Alphonse a simple test: Wear the Miraculous Medal and repeat the Memorare each morning.

While Alphonse didn't initially like the idea, he finally agreed to it. Meanwhile, the baron asked several of his friends to pray for Alphonse. One of these friends was a count who was very ill. The count prayed twenty Memorares for Alphonse's conversion on the very day he passed away. The next day, the baron was arranging the count's funeral and asked Alphonse to accompany him. While the baron spoke with the priest, Alphonse wandered through the church looking at the art. That's when something unusual happened. Alphonse later recalled:

> *I was scarcely in the church when a total confusion came over me. When I looked up, it seemed to me that the entire church had been swallowed up in shadow, except one chapel. It was as though all the light was concentrated in that single place. I looked over towards this chapel whence so much light shone, and above the altar was a living figure, tall, majestic, beautiful, and full of mercy. It was the most holy Virgin Mary, resembling her figure on the Miraculous Medal. At this sight I fell on my knees right where I stood. Unable to look up because of the blinding light, I fixed my glance on her hands, and in them I could read the expression of mercy and pardon. In the presence of the Most Blessed Virgin, even though she did not speak a word to me, I understood the frightful situation I was in, my sins, and the beauty of the Catholic Faith.*

The baron returned from his meeting and was surprised to see Alphonse fervently praying on his knees before the altar of St. Michael the Archangel. As they walked back to Alphonse's hotel, the young man held on tightly to his miraculous medal. He was sobbing and between cries would murmur shouts of thanksgiving to God. Then he turned to the baron, hugged him, and said, "Take me to a confessor! When can I receive baptism, without which I can no longer live?" The baron asked what he saw, but Alphonse demanded a priest. The two quickly walked to the Gesu, the mother church of the Jesuits. Alphonse could barely explain himself through his tears. Finally, when he calmed down enough, he took off his Miraculous Medal, held it up, and cried, "I saw her! I saw her!" Eleven days later, he received Baptism, Confirmation, and First Communion.

Both the miracle and Alphonse's conversion were a shock to the aristocratic society of Europe. More and more people were turning against the Church. Many had accepted philosophies that encouraged strictly rational thought and the denial of the divine and miraculous. The following month, the Vatican held lengthy investigations surrounding Alphonse's conversion. They concluded that his sudden conversion was entirely miraculous.

Alphonse entered the Jesuit order after his conversion and became a priest, just like his brother. He spent the rest of his life working alongside his brother. He died on May 6, 1884.

DAY 28 REFLECTION & MEDITATION

St. Ignatius of Loyola, the founder of the Jesuits, wrote a beautiful prayer called the Suscipe, inviting us to give God everything we have. Pray this prayer now and then share with God whatever is on your heart.

> *Take, Lord, and receive all my liberty, my memory, my understanding, and my entire will,*
> *All I have and call my own.*
> *You have given all to me.*
> *To you, Lord, I return it.*
> *Everything is yours; do with it what you will.*
> *Give me only your love and your grace, that is enough for me. Amen.*

DAY 29 WE KNOW HE'S A SAINT

WE KNOW HE'S A SAINT

It is only through suffering that we become holy. And to become holy is our only purpose in life, our only preparation for heaven.
• BLESSED FRANCIS XAVIER SEELOS •

In 1965, Angela Boudreaux, a wife and mother of four, was hospitalized because her liver was nine times the normal size. After additional surgeries and tests, doctors found her liver was almost entirely replaced by cancer. They told Angela that she would most likely die of total liver failure within two weeks.

Despite the dire diagnosis, Angela didn't begin planning her funeral. Instead, she turned to a priest who recently had greatly impacted her family.

Angela's young son, John, had developed severe eczema. The toddler scratched and bled, screaming and crying at all hours of the day and night for almost a year. Exhausted and helpless, Angela heard about Fr. Francis Xavier Seelos, a Redemptorist priest who had died one hundred years earlier. Angela's family prayed for Fr. Seelos's intercession, and they soon found a medical cure for John. Having just experienced this healing power five months earlier, Angela turned to Fr. Seelos once again.

Francis Xavier Seelos was born in 1819 to a large Catholic family in Bavaria, Germany. From a very young age, Francis had a deep and unwavering faith. He was also full of fun and loved making his friends and family happy. In 1843, he joined the Redemptorist order and was sent to the United States. Very quickly, his order and those whom he served recognized his sanctity. One of his bishops remarked, "One only has to look at him to know he is a saint."

From the beginning of his ministry, Fr. Seelos was renowned for his gift of healing. His gift became so well-known that a crippled man once came and told him, "I'm not leaving until you cure me." When Fr. Seelos prayed the Church's blessing for the sick, the man felt a strange feeling pass through his crippled legs, and he began to walk.

In the fall of 1867, the city of New Orleans experienced an outbreak of yellow fever, and Fr. Seelos became one of the many victims. Incredible miracles surrounded his passing and continued after his death by those who asked for his intercession.

It was to this man that Angela now turned in her most desperate moments.

Somehow, after her prayers to Fr. Seelos, Angela started improving—so much so that she was released from the hospital. Eventually, doctors recommended an experimental drug. They told Angela that she would have to lie flat on her back for an entire year and would experience extreme side effects such as nausea, hair loss, and bleeding gums.

Angela continued her prayers to Fr. Seelos, and to the great surprise of her doctors, Angela showed no side effects after receiving the experimental drug. Only four months later, she was up and about, hosting guests at her home and preparing meals for the holidays. Over time, she made a complete recovery. In spite of the drug, doctors were absolutely convinced that her recovery was a miracle. She lived on far longer than expected even before taking the drug, and her liver healed too rapidly for chemotherapy to be the cause of her recovery.

Angela's miracle was submitted to the Vatican for the cause for Fr. Seelos' canonization. In the year 2000, Angela attended the beatification with her family as the official recipient of his beatification miracle.

Yet Angela and her son John weren't the only members of the family who received healings through Fr. Seelos's intercession. The Boudreaux family attributes a total of five dramatic healings of various kinds to this saintly man.

DAY 29 REFLECTION & MEDITATION

As you reflect on the life of Bl. Francis Xavier Seelos, take a few moments to think of something you need healing for. Who else in your life might benefit from the intercession of this holy saint? Pray for them now.

SACRED HEART

I need nothing but God, and to lose myself in the heart of Jesus.
• ST. MARGARET MARY ALACOQUE •

Margaret Mary Alacoque was born in 1647 in Burgundy, France. Her father died when she was just eight years old, and the family fell into poverty when her father's trustee unjustly withheld his estate from them.

In addition to this suffering, Margaret Mary became ill with rheumatic fever, leaving her bedridden for four years. When she miraculously recovered, her family—who had managed to recover their property—introduced Margaret Mary to the glamorous life of a young socialite. No longer ill, Margaret Mary became swept up in the delights and pleasures of the world. But after seeing a vision of Jesus' scourging at the pillar, she was reminded of the vow she had made as a young child to become a nun, and she chose to honor it.

In her early years as a nun, she was kept busy working in the convent's infirmary. She also found true solace and joy in spending many hours with Jesus in prayer.

Then, in 1673, everything changed.

While she was praying in adoration before the Blessed Sacrament, Margaret Mary heard Jesus speaking to her. He told her that He wanted to spread the love of His heart through her and that she would reveal to many people the grace He desired to bestow on humanity. In this vision, Margaret Mary saw Jesus take her heart and place it within His, setting it aflame with divine love that continued to burn in her heart as it returned to her body.

Over the next eighteen months, Jesus continued to appear to Margaret Mary, explaining in detail the desire of His heart to be honored in the devotion we now know as the "Sacred Heart."

In a letter, Margaret Mary described the Sacred Heart as "an abyss of all blessings." She wrote:

Into it the poor should submerge all their needs. It is an abyss of joy in which all of us can immerse our sorrows. It is an abyss of lowliness to counteract our foolishness, an abyss of mercy for the wretched, an abyss of love to meet our every need.

Margaret Mary endured many sufferings because of these visions. Theologians and Church authorities refused to believe her. Many of her fellow sisters did not believe her either and accused her of lying to get attention. But when the Jesuit priest Fr. Claude de la Colombière was chosen as the confessor for her convent, he listened to Margaret Mary describe her visions and declared them authentic. Though it would take seventy-five years for the devotion to the Sacred Heart to be officially recognized by the Catholic Church, the beautiful image and message began to spread.

In the years following her visions, Margaret Mary grew weaker and weaker, but the divine flame of love never ceased to burn in her heart. As she lay dying in 1690, Margaret Mary said: "I need nothing but God, and to lose myself in the heart of Jesus."

Margaret Mary was canonized in 1920. Her confessor, Fr. Claude, was canonized a saint as well in 1992.

While the visions Margaret Mary Alacoque received were miraculous, the widespread love of Jesus' Sacred Heart points to the goodness of God working through this humble nun for the blessing of all.

DAY 30 REFLECTION & MEDITATION

Pray a prayer today to the Sacred Heart of Jesus:

O most holy Heart of Jesus, fountain of every blessing,
I adore you, I love you, and with a lively sorrow for my sins,
I offer you this poor heart of mine.
Make me humble, patient, pure, and wholly obedient to your will.
Grant, good Jesus, that I may live in you and for you.
Protect me in the midst of danger; comfort me in my afflictions;
give me health of body, assistance in my temporal needs,
your blessings on all that I do, and the grace of a holy death.
Within your heart I place my every care.
In every need let me come to you with humble trust saying,
Heart of Jesus, help me. Amen.

Like St. Margaret Mary Alocoque, rest in the Sacred Heart of Jesus. Let Him enflame your heart with His divine love.

DAY 31 INTERRUPTED

INTERRUPTED

"Do not fear, only believe."
• JESUS' WORDS TO JAIRUS •

Jairus, a synagogue official, waited impatiently, his heart pounding. He had approached Jesus and begged him to come save his daughter from death, and Jesus agreed. Then, as they were on their way, Jesus stopped to turn to a woman in rags. Jairus saw him speak to her. Saw him hold her hand and listen as she talked to him. He saw her face light up with the biggest smile, and he saw Jesus look back at her with love.

But every moment was agonizing. Every moment brought his beloved little daughter closer to death. *Please, God*, he thought, *please hurry. Please don't let us be too late.*

Jesus finally turned back to Jairus, and Jairus felt his heart swell with hope. But then he saw people from his house making their way over to him. He knew what they were going to say before they said it. His daughter was dead.

They were too late.

The miracle that day belonged to the needy woman, not to him and not to his daughter. They had been *so close*. Just a few more minutes, a few more steps, and perhaps Jesus would have made it in time.

But Jesus seems unperturbed. "Do not be afraid," he said to the newly bereaved father. "Just believe."

Just believe? Jairus felt anger rise in his heart. His faith was why he threw himself at the feet of Jesus in the first place, pleading for help and healing. And what good had that belief done for him?

But he followed Jesus anyway. Mostly because, well . . . what did he have to lose? But also, deep down, there was still the smallest bit of hope in his heart. If Jesus really was who so many said he was, maybe he could bring his daughter back.

They continued down the road to Jairus's home where his relatives were weeping and wailing, mourning the little girl.

Jesus turned to them. "The child is not dead," he assured them. "She is not dead, but asleep."

They laughed bitterly at Jesus. "Jairus, can you believe this man? I know it's hard to take, but she isn't just sleeping. Don't put yourself through any more pain."

But Jairus looked only at Jesus. He held on to that small amount of hope and didn't let it go. He took his wife's hand, and they followed Jesus into the house.

They went into the room where their daughter was lying motionless. Jesus knelt beside her bed. He took her hand and said to her, "Little girl, arise."

Her eyes flickered open. Jairus' eyes filled with tears as he watched her sit up and smile at them. She got out of bed, walked over to her parents, and hugged them.

She was whole and healthy and *alive*!

DAY 31 REFLECTION & MEDITATION

Have you felt like Jairus at times—caught between the faith-filled hope that Jesus will answer your prayers and the human fear that help might never come? Have you ever wondered: where is my miracle? Why should others' prayers be answered but not mine?

Bring to God now any miracles you are waiting on, any unanswered prayers or hopes. Share with Him anything that is on your heart (even any anger or questions you might have). Rest in the peace He offers each of us.

DAY 32 THE MOST EXTRAORDINARY PERSON

THE MOST EXTRAORDINARY PERSON

One life is all we have and we live it as we believe in living it. But to sacrifice what you are and to live without belief, that is a fate more terrible than dying.
· ST. JOAN OF ARC ·

Mark Twain once said that St. Joan of Arc "is easily and by far the most extraordinary person the human race has ever produced." Many historians agree with him. Joan of Arc is best remembered for leading a failing French army to one of the most unexpected military victories in history. She was not only uneducated, something that would have greatly discredited her ability to lead an army at that time, but she was also a woman in the army, something that was unheard of in medieval Christianity. Oh, and she was also a teenager.

In order for her to be in the position to lead an army, much less be able to obtain a monumental and unexpected victory at such a young age, something truly remarkable would need to happen. In the case of Joan, *several* miraculous events occurred.

Joan of Arc was born in 1412 in northeastern France to a peasant family in a mountain village. At the time, France was engaged with England in the Hundred Years' War. When Joan was thirteen, she began to receive visions from God. In particular, St. Catherine, St. Michael, and St. Margaret all appeared to her. They told her to drive the English out of France and to see that the French dauphin, the future Charles VII, be crowned the true king of France in Reims. The only problem: Reims, like much of France at the time, was currently occupied by the English.

At the age of seventeen, Joan appeared by herself at a local fort and asked the captain of the guard to take her to Charles, the dauphin. They laughed at her and dismissed her. Accompanied by her cousin, she later returned with the same request and received a similar welcome. To prove herself, Joan prophesied that the town of Orleans would fall. To everyone's shock, her prediction came true, and the garrison commander, Robert de Baudricourt, agreed to escort her to the dauphin.

News of Joan spread, and the future King Charles devised a plan upon her arrival. Amid the many people in his court, he disguised himself and placed another person in his place on the throne. Although she had never seen Charles before, Joan recognized him immediately. Then, in a conversation with Charles, she revealed the details of a private prayer he had made to God to save France. In time, Charles would allow her to lead the French soldiers into battle, and through a number of improbable victories, Joan's forces routed the English, paving the way for the unthinkable—the crowning of Charles as king of France in Reims.

After this time, Joan was captured in battle, turned over to the English, and tried as a heretic. Despite her young age and no theological training, she was able to outwit the top theologians in England—so much so that the trial was eventually made private rather than public to spare them from embarrassment. Because of their prejudices and fear, these theologians declared Joan guilty of heresy, and she was burned at the stake at the age of nineteen. Later, an investigation into her trial was made, and Joan was declared innocent of all charges and designated a martyr. She was canonized a saint in 1920 and named the patron saint of France.

DAY 32 REFLECTION & MEDITATION

St. Joan of Arc placed her faith above all else. In what areas of your life does your faith come second? How is God calling you to trust in Him more? How can your faith impact your actions today?

DAY 33 MIRACLE MAN OF MONTREAL

MIRACLE MAN OF MONTREAL

Therefore I am content with weaknesses, insults, hardships, persecutions, and calamities for the sake of Christ; for whenever I am weak, then I am strong.

• 2 CORINTHIANS 12:10 •

In Montreal, Canada, a magnificent church sits on a hilltop. Hundreds of crutches cover the walls of the crypt inside, crutches that were cast off after healings occurred. But before it was a great church, it was a simple structure built by a humble man whose only desire was to bring more people to Jesus through the prayers of St. Joseph. This is his story.

When Alfred was born in 1845 in Canada, no one thought he would live very long. He was sickly his entire childhood, and he lost both his parents by the age of twelve. He had to work to support himself, and so he received very little education. Throughout these sufferings, however, his love of Jesus only grew, and he desired to enter religious life.

When his childhood pastor sent Alfred to join the Congregation of the Holy Cross, he wrote them a note that said: "I am sending you a saint." Upon entering the Congregation of the Holy Cross, Alfred took the name André. Given his frail health and lack of formal education, Brother André was assigned as doorkeeper of Notre Dame College in Montreal. He desired to spread devotion to St. Joseph, so he saved the money he earned from giving haircuts to construct a simple structure, known as the Oratory—or Chapel—of St. Joseph.

As doorkeeper of the college, Brother André interacted with the students and teachers and listened to their problems. He would pray for them and instruct them to seek the intercession of St. Joseph. People soon realized that when Brother André prayed for a person in need, they were healed. Word spread, and more and more people began to seek out Brother Andre. He would often greet those with physical ailments with the words, "There is nothing wrong with you!"

Brother André's ministry for the rest of his life was to receive the long lines of sick visitors who flocked to St. Joseph's Oratory, where a basilica was built to replace the small chapel. He became known as the "Miracle Man of Montreal." Brother André would laugh at this and say, "It is St. Joseph who does these things; I am, like you, simply a suppliant."

Over ten thousand people have been cured, with some estimates reaching as many as 125,000. Here are just two of them:

A nineteen-month-old child swallowed lye, burning her mouth and throat to the point where she could only take a few drops of milk at a time through a tube. Br. Andre simply said she would be healed, and she was.

Twenty-two-year-old Joseph Jette was paralyzed for life after falling from some scaffolding. He was carried to Br. André, and Joseph recalled: "He ordered me to put down my crutches and walk. I obeyed. I was cured!"

When Brother André died at age ninety-one, more than a million people braved the cold Canadian winter to pay their respects at St. Joseph's Oratory. He was canonized in 2010.

DAY 33 REFLECTION & MEDITATION

St. André's story reminds us that God works in unexpected ways, often using our weakness for His glory if we are open to letting Him work through us. St. André's humble life mirrored the humble life of his patron, St. Joseph.

Is there anyone you know who lives a humble life but radiates God's presence to others in a tangible way? How do you see God using your ordinary life for His glory? Thank Him for being strong when you are weak, and trust Him to shine through you.

During the last thirty-three days, we've looked at various miracle stories from Scripture and the history of the Church. The whole goal of this journey was to recognize that if God is alive, it changes everything. We hope that these stories have encouraged you, challenged you, and opened your eyes to the ways God works in your own life. Thank you for joining us in this time together. Feel free to go back to any miracle stories that particularly inspired you or share them with others. May God bless you!

Meditate on These Miracles and More

ON HALLOW, #1 CATHOLIC APP

Daily Rosary with Mark Wahlberg, Bishop Barron, and more.

Bible & Catechism in a Year with Fr. Mike

Exclusive Community Prayer Challenges such as Advent Feat. *The Chosen*

MARK WAHLBERG

Come, Holy Spirit

Advent #P
featuring T

Join the Hallow commu
journey through the stor
God's chosen people in

250,000 PRAYING

In the Begi
Day 1 with John

Adam and
Day 2 with Johr

Noah
Day 3 with Johr

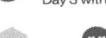

Home   Meditate

NOTES